THE LATCH KEY KID

– A Memoir of Anhedonia –

By

M.J. HUGHES

DEDICATION

Dedicated to all the Latch Key Kids around the world.

CONTENTS

AUTHOR'S NOTE

For the sake of my children, for those who love me, and for those who grew up with me and who have no control over me retelling our story, most names in this book have been changed. But this is a true story and, allowing for the inaccuracies of memory over time, every event you're about to read of took place as depicted and made me who I am.

INTRODUCTION

There is a name for what I have. A name that explains my behaviour and describes, in exact detail, the things that are wrong with me.

These things have been wrong with me all my life and, having a name for them, a condition with a title, doesn't change how I am. I am still me. The guy down the pub who won't talk to you about football, or *Coronation Street*, or William and Kate, or Page Three. If I visit your home, I won't get any enjoyment from the food you cook, I won't get excited by your new gas barbeque with its searing rods and rotisserie burner, and I won't cuddle up to your dog. Even if you tell me it cost you the best part of a grand, I won't be impressed. If you work with me, I won't ask you about your weekend on a Monday morning, or tell you about mine, or take you out at dinnertime, or think to put the radio on when it's quiet so we can have a sing-song. I won't do any of that.

I am Mike Hughes, and I have been diagnosed with anhedonia.

Never heard of it? Neither had I.

1

The word comes from the French *anhédonie*, which itself comes from the Greek *an-* (meaning 'without', or 'lacking') and *hēdoné* (meaning 'pleasure'). An inability to experience pleasure. It is categorised as a psychological condition and is often experienced by those who are depressed.

For me, however, it's a bit different. You see, this is a lifelong condition and it's never caused me to get depressed, because I don't actually experience any kind of emotion at all – not happiness or sadness, or anything in between.

Lee Child put it well in his *Make Me* novel starring Jack Reacher, in which missing Michael suffers from anhedonia: 'Depressed means what it says, which is pushed down below the normal position. Which implies a range. Which Michael doesn't have.' Child refers to it as a 'happiness meter stuck on zero', and it's true: I don't go above zero on the emotional scale, and I don't go below. I have never felt pleasure or enjoyment, so how could I possibly feel the depths of such despair?

Since learning this name – 'anhedonia' – I have discovered a few other sufferers through forums and blogs on the internet. But not many. And that's probably because of the very nature of anhedonia itself: deep down we might see that we're emotionally different from everyone else, but we just accept that this is the way we are, giving it no further thought. We're not *interested* in finding out why. We would never think to discuss it with a friend or family member – what good would that do? And we wouldn't go to see a doctor or psychiatrist, as that would involve some kind of emotional decision – a *want* to change yourself, a *desire* to be different, a *need* to know what's wrong – and wants, desires and needs aren't what someone with anhedonia experiences. The only reason I was diagnosed with anhedonia is because I began studying psychotherapy and that training, one way or another, led me to talk to Dr Greenberg, an American psychotherapist. Until these sessions with Dr Greenberg, I didn't realise my distinctive personality traits were 'symptoms'. I just accepted the way I was and I got on with it.

The zero level of emotional engagement means I have no interest in anything. I mean nothing. And I never have. Not food, or drink, or drugs, or sex, or clothes, or travel, or music, or sport, or politics, or business, or finance, or anything else you can imagine. If there's nothing I'm required to do, I can sit for hours, even days, just waiting, the TV on in the background, a book in my hand. Great for airport delays, not so great for getting ahead in life. This neutral state spreads to every corner of my existence: to find the best line of work for yourself, you need to have an interest in something, anything; to save money, you need to have an interest in the thing you're saving for; to go down the pub, you need to have an interest in talking to people, or drinking; to make friends, you need to have an interest in others; to feel angry, you need to have an interest in whatever it is you're fighting for or about; to feel sexy, you need to have an interest in sex; to love someone, you need to have an interest in affection and closeness. To feel any kind of drive, or motivation, you need to have an interest in whatever it is you're going to do. For someone with anhedonia, there is no interest.

Basically, you could easily mistake me for a miserable sod.

*

You might have put two and two together and realised that, thanks to my lack of emotional recognition, this book is not about gaining sympathy. While you could find some of what follows distressing or upsetting (so others tell me), to me, your sympathy is a waste of time: what good does feeling sorry for me do? Will it benefit either of us? It's not a practical response to a situation, therefore, it doesn't compute with me. No, I've written this book as a guide to a mental health condition that isn't widely understood. Most people have never heard of anhedonia and those I talk to about it find it incredibly hard to get on board with the idea.

There have been huge awareness campaigns to highlight mental health issues, because people don't see them and so can't comprehend what it's like. I still hear sufferers of depression being told to 'cheer up'; it's ridiculous! And it's this lack of understanding that brings about the same response when I try to explain anhedonia:

'You enjoy football, though?' they say.

'No, I don't.'

'Well, you must enjoy music?'

'No, I don't.'

'How about spending time with your friends?'

'Nope. Don't enjoy that either.'

'I know you enjoy my company…?'

'No, no – I don't…'

I want people to understand how different my life is from theirs without that emotional range to guide what I do, and I want to show you how you take those little decisions, made every hour of every day, for granted. I also want to see if I can help someone else who recognises themselves in my personality; show them there's a reason for how they are, a reason for why they don't feel. Although I have never cared about anything, it's always been hard to understand why I don't have the reactions of everyone else. 'Anhedonia' gives me an explanation for why I am how I am. And this makes my life easier. I no longer have to try and explain something that's inexplicable, to myself, or to anyone else. I can simply say, instead: 'It's anhedonia. And if you don't know what that means, read this book.'

1

ANHEDONIC LIFE

Dr Greenberg: Please answer 'yes' or 'no' to the following questions, and be as honest as you can. Do you think that you could be content living alone in a cabin in the woods?

Everything I have learnt about psychology and psychoanalysis indicates that each of us is born the same, ready to be moulded by the lives we lead. Therefore, logically, I wasn't born without emotion. But, saying that, I don't ever remember not being like this. Part of me thinks my mum might have had anhedonia too – I never saw her properly smile or laugh, she took no pride in my sister and me, didn't show any admiration towards us – so maybe it could be genetic. Or maybe I was just born this way.

It doesn't really matter where it came from, because this is how I've always been and I've learnt to cope with it, and how to act like a normal person in everyday life.

Fitting in with other people has always been important to me. Not because I want close friendships – I don't really like talking to people – but because there are practical benefits to having people around who like me. When I was a kid, I'd give a lad a bag of penny sweets, knowing that he'd like the sweets and so later that day would invite me round for tea. Nowadays, it's more about getting business deals, or a good seat in a restaurant.

I'm opening up a can of worms by writing this, exposing my camouflage completely to those who know me, or who have ever met me, but: in order to appear like a normal human being, I become a kind of chameleon when I'm put in a social situation, mimicking your behaviour, matching your body language, feigning interest in your interests, copying your style of conversation, all to look like I'm not completely emotionally void.

As soon as I meet someone new, I try to pick up on something they're interested in and give them a random fact that's related. You're reading this book so it's safe to assume you have an interest in books: did you know, apparently it takes an average of 475 hours to write a novel (almost three months, if you're working to 40-hour weeks)? Look at that, it seems like we have a common interest that we can now discuss. Believe me, we don't have a common interest. But that's not your fault.

If we're likely to be talking for a while, say at a dinner party (something I try to avoid, by the way), I'll do my best to lead the conversation on to your upbringing, or religion, or the state of the world. I'm able to deal with intense conversations far more easily than chitchat about football or soap stars, because there's no practical need for anyone to know about hat tricks, or Sharon Whatsit on *EastEnders*. To me, deep conversations are practical: both of us might learn something that we can apply to another area of life.

To try and hide my lack of emotion, I become this social chameleon, acting and talking in a way that's expected of me. Basically, by mimicking your emotions, I can be highly likeable because I appear just like you, if not exactly like you (after all, there is no 'me' for you to get to know). This, however, is extremely draining. Especially if the person has a large ego. If you're a bit down or shy, my mood will seem appropriately sombre or calm, but if you're loud and arrogant, then that's what I'll be, giving good banter, just like you. If you're upbeat and laughing, I'll be upbeat and laughing. It's not real laughter, but you'll think it is. If you're annoyed, I'll be annoyed along with you, or if you're excited, I'll seem excitable as well – though I can't sustain it for very long. I've never understood excitement as an emotion: why does someone get excited at a pop concert, or even at the radio, when a sad song comes on? It just sounds depressing to me, so why don't you feel depressed? It's the same when people get excited at a goal in a football match. I think, *Are these screaming people alright? Do they need some medication?* It's baffling. But I do understand that they're having the usual reaction, and I'm not.

Occasionally, I experience 'flickers' of emotion. They're over as quickly as a car passing by, but I do get them now and again. For half a second I might find something funny, I might feel just a bit irritable, or even disappointed. But it's over as soon as it's started. If I ever got in a fight as a kid, that first push might have seemed right, but then I would suddenly forget the feeling and either imitate what I thought my mates would do in the same situation (faking aggression so that I didn't lose face), or I'd just walk away, confusing the other lad entirely. These flickers don't happen often and are usually the result of an extreme situation, with something that's very funny or annoying. Now and then, I also experience flickers from other people, especially children or women in distress. I feel like I have an almost spiritual empathy for them and can draw on their emotions. When each of my kids was born, I cradled them in my arms and felt that safety that they felt from my nurturing: a kind of warmth. It's like I'm stealing their emotions, rather than experiencing my own.

As you may well be able to imagine, having anhedonia can create a very solitary existence. If I'm not making a massive effort, I can come across as abrupt. My answers to questions are often vague or single-worded, and apparently can sound quite rude, maybe even harsh. I don't mean to be, but I sometimes forget that other people have emotional responses. You see, nothing ever offends me. And I really do mean nothing. While I never want to upset anyone, it's hard to get my head around the fact that other people can be incredibly sensitive, about the words I use, the answers I give to problems, the responses I have to illness and death. I basically don't have a filter. And it gets me into trouble. The other day someone was telling me about their neighbour's son who was hit by a train in rush hour. My response, without thinking, was a practical one: 'That must have been a bugger for everyone going to work.' I'm not being insensitive and making a bad-taste joke, I just genuinely, automatically think about the practicalities of every situation, because I don't have the emotions for anything else. This means that to put up with the real me, you have to have a pretty tolerant attitude. There's actually only one person I've ever managed to keep, what *you* might call, a 'friendship' with over a long period of time. And that's Shirl – aka Cohen the Barbarian – a biker bloke who randomly saved my neck when I was in my early twenties, and who I then met again ten years ago. I don't mind going for a pint with Shirl every couple of weeks because I can be myself with him; he tolerates my bluntness, or rudeness, or whatever you want to call it, because I don't expect anything from him, and I tolerate his miserable cantankerousness because he doesn't expect a single thing from me either. But Shirl is a rarity in my life. Generally I have to put in a hell of a lot of effort when I'm with other people.

When I am making an effort – playing the game of being nice – I'll be very careful with my responses, aware of every word I use. I had a meeting with a guy just this week who I'd never met before, and straight away he looked all six-foot-two of me up and down and said: 'My God, I wouldn't want to cross you.'

I grinned and said: 'Don't worry about me, I'm a teddy bear.'

In that split second, I came across like I have emotions: grinning, giving a bit of humour (something I turn to a lot), telling him not to worry, softening him with the image of a toy. And, most importantly, not evoking any other kind of response in him other than a brief chuckle, therefore ending this farce and letting us get on with business.

Because I'm so reassuring and approachable, and I mimic behaviours, people genuinely like spending time with me. But when I turn down their invitations to spend more time with them, they soon go off me. In all honesty, I don't like spending time with other people, to the extent that if I make a lot of friends in one place, like down the pub, I'll avoid ever going back. I feel more secure on my own, taking care of myself, and I have never experienced a desire to make an attachment with another person, unless there's a clear, practical reason to do so. Since the age of about three, I have been independent, and even back then I never craved any attention from my mum. Like me, she certainly wasn't warm and affectionate. But the way she acted with me was normal, in my eyes. I was used to our relationship and didn't expect – or want – anything else from her. It's only now, when my wife points out how I wouldn't want my children treated in the way I was, that I see things weren't right with how Mum raised me. And so I make the effort to be affectionate with my kids.

You might wonder, when I don't like the company of other people, how it is that I'm married and have children. I might not experience love and attachment to another person in the same way that you do, but I can see the good in people and my wife is the most kind and caring woman I've ever come across. She's a good influence on me and I married her because I seriously couldn't imagine that anyone better than her exists in the world.

The anhedonia gives me some good husband-material attributes: supportive, loyal, and most importantly, honest – lies are emotional responses, therefore I don't lie; I really don't see the point. But while there are good sides to my personality, close relationships are always difficult for me. This is mainly because I have literally no emotional engagement. I can't keep up my social chameleon act 24/7, so my partner sees the raw version of me, and that can cause all sorts of problems, big and small.

Just imagine living with someone who is always honest and not interested in anything. What would you do if your partner didn't flinch when there was a devastatingly sad scene on the news, would you find it weird, disturbing maybe?

Would it be okay if your partner said exactly – honestly – what they thought of your new outfit? Would not ever hearing the words 'I love you' get you down? Would you find it acceptable if your partner completely lacked sympathy when someone close to you died? None of this is deliberate, I don't try to be awkward, and I don't intend to be mean, but I have no natural emotion to help me behave appropriately in any of these situations when they catch me off guard. When I'm at home, just like everyone, I'm more myself: my wife gets the blunt, un-sugar-coated me. Being this way has meant that three of the women I have had serious relationships with have used the exact same phrase to describe me: *you don't have a heart, you have a swinging brick.*

And then there's sex. To me, sex is chemical rather than emotional: the same as anyone, I experience the chemical reaction, the endorphins releasing to make you feel good; I just don't get that physical *need* to have sex. When I'm in a long-term relationship, once I've made a connection with the woman I'm with, then I don't mind having sex at all. But I could never sleep with a person I didn't know. When I was younger, my mates would sleep with any girl who said yes. They had a *need*, a *desire* for sex, for that physical release; they wanted it more than anything. I've never had that. I have to get to know a woman first, let those chemicals inside make a natural connection, before I can sleep with her.

When I was single, women tended to warm to me very easily, without me doing anything, and I think that's because I never tried it on with them, because sex wasn't on my mind. Instead of attempting to get in their knickers, I'd listen to their problems, have deep conversations with them and try to help them through their issues. This wasn't a crafty pulling technique. It was just my way of fitting into society; I still do it with both men and women.

Without emotions getting in the way of my thinking, I'm able to see practical solutions to problems clearly and easily. I used to talk to people down the pub about their childhood traumas, severe stresses in their lives, or their states of depression. It's amazing what a pint can do for opening people up, and I earned myself the nickname Preacher for these boozy psychotherapy sessions. It was something I could do to help people, and it didn't cost me or them a penny.

Don't assume I was doing all this out of the goodness of my heart. The practical side for me was that helping someone meant a bit of good karma –

something I very much believe in.

There was a woman from Thailand, Piti, who used to come in the pub a lot, and she had a severe gag reflex that meant she struggled to even brush her teeth. Piti had no clue what the reason behind this was and she felt quite desperate about the situation. I took her to one side and started talking to her, trying to uncover a significant emotional event that might have impacted her psyche.

After a very short time, she began telling me of when she was a toddler, growing up in a house by the ocean. Piti's older siblings were allowed to run out to the cliff edge and dive the short distance down into the sea, but she was never permitted to join them, being too young to swim. While her siblings were outside, her mother would stand at the kitchen window, watching them intently and wouldn't pay Piti any mind. Piti, young and desperate for her mother's attention, would jump around and dance, but her mother would ignore her. So, one day, in a bid to get attention, Piti ran out to the cliff after her brother and sisters and, before her mother could stop her, she dived off the edge into the sea. Of course, being so young, she couldn't swim and almost drowned. She was saved by one of the older children, but the struggle to breathe that she felt whilst being revived, left her with this strange gag reflex that had lasted right into adulthood. This was a memory she hadn't revisited since, yet after this one conversation she found her gag reflex had gone completely. She and I faced the trauma from her childhood and we processed it all as rational adults, allowing her to put it to bed.

Though I don't have the capacity to experience emotions myself, other people's emotions are very clear to me, making me intuitive when it comes to their problems.

But I'm a bit like a diode, in which electricity flows one way and not the other: I'll do things to help people, because I can. It's something to do. But I don't want anyone to do anything for me. I'm fine to cope on my own. In fact, I prefer looking after my own well-being.

The trouble with letting other people in is that they will suddenly want to ask a lot of questions about a lot of things – from why I feel a certain way, to whether I want a cup of tea – and answering questions makes me very nervous. Consider how you form an answer to a normal question in everyday life and you'll realise that it comes from a basic emotional level. Especially answers to simple questions.

Question: Would you like to go for a walk with me?

Average person: [Thinks* *I do like going for walks, but right now I'm comfortable in this chair.*] No, but thank you for the offer.

Me: [Thinks* *I don't know if I'd like to go for a walk or not.*

Do I like walks? I don't know. Do most people like walks? I don't not *like going for walks, so I probably do like walks. I don't mind sitting here, though. But, then again, I don't think anything bad will happen if I go for a walk. There's a reason they're asking me to go for a walk, which means if I say 'no' they'll probably*

ask why I don't want to go for a walk and I don't have a reason not to go, and they might get upset if I don't go because they've asked me to go and I can't say why I won't go, so I should probably just go for a walk…]
Yes, please.

Because I've been this way for as long as I can remember – as far back as my early childhood – I've learnt that 'yes' is usually the best answer to most questions. It's the easiest answer to please people, to not offend people or hurt their feelings, and to avoid that battle in my head of whether I like/want something or not.

As a forty-six-year-old man with a lot of life experience, I now have a moral compass to help guide my answers. I quickly judge whether there will be a bad outcome from my 'yes' answer – whether it could end with me in prison, or someone getting hurt – and if I can't see a negative result, I say, 'Yes.' When I was younger, however, I didn't have anyone to guide me in what was right and wrong, I had no idea what I should be saying 'no' to and I couldn't foresee the repercussions of my actions.

There's no way on earth I would now say 'yes' if someone asked me to hold a shotgun for them and point it in the direction of a bank cashier; I don't want to go to prison and I don't want to accidentally shoot someone, or mentally scar them for life. As a teenager, though, I would have made a split-second decision in that scenario – a coin toss in my head, thinking only of the current moment, not the future – and there would have been a strong chance I would have said, 'Okay,' because I couldn't instantly see a reason not to. My thinking went like this: my mate has asked me to do something, so it must be fine for me to do it, else why would he ask? Thankfully, no one ever asked me to hold a gun and I learnt to stay away from those kinds of people, eventually.

The experience of anhedonia means I see things in a black and white way, so decisions I make don't always make sense to other people. My brain hears a problem; my brain relentlessly searches for a practical solution; and my mind can't rest until a decision is made. Because I have no emotions to get in the way of my decision-making, everything gets simplified to an absolute, basic practical level.

I've just lost my job = Well, get another one. One hundred per cent of my focus is now on getting a new job.

My wife is cheating on me = Leave her. I pack my bags and go immediately.

There's no fussing with arguments or trying to work things out.

I need a new car = Buy one outright; that one will do. I could easily afford a Porsche on credit, but why spend thirty thousand, when you can spend three?

I once hired a man who, only the week before, had punched all my front teeth out because I'd started seeing his ex-girlfriend. Unlike a lot of other people who would hold a grudge against him, maybe want revenge and have him beaten up, I understood that he punched me – several times – because he wanted to be with his ex-girlfriend. It made sense to me that he would hit me out of frustration, an inability to cope with his emotions. Why would that then stop me giving him a job, especially when I needed someone, and he needed work? It's a black and white way of thinking, but it makes complete sense. To me.

The more serious a problem is, the easier it is for me to make a decision. Without having emotions to confuse things, I can clearly – and quickly – weigh up the practicalities of every angle. I truly believe that people with anhedonia have to be very clever (myself included), because we're constantly trying to analyse situations from *practical*, not emotional, standpoints: rapidly taking into account a series of outcomes, determining what the best course of action is, reanalysing to ensure it's correct, and deciding on the best solution, all in just the blink of an eye. It's if I'm faced with a simple question that I find it incredibly hard to make a decision. *What would you like for tea?* = I really don't care. *Where would you like to go tomorrow?* = I really don't care.

But, once I do make a decision to do something serious, I'm then faced with an internal battle over whether to continue or not. If there's an obvious, practical reason to carry on – like the time I ripped my bathroom out, there was no going back then – it's easy to decide to continue. However, if it's more of a choice that I've made – studying psychotherapy, say – then I will keep weighing up the options, over and over, convinced that I'm wasting my time and that another let-down is around the corner. Eventually, sick of this mental back and forth, I'll usually come up with the following solution: 'Oh well, I've come this far, I might as well keep going.' It's not like I'll start another project or task and get pleasure from that, so what else can I do other than finish what I start? The trouble is, I'll have this battle with myself over anything I take on, whether it's painting the dining table, buying a motorbike, or even writing this book.

*

According to my wife, a lot of bad stuff has happened to me in my life. A lot of stuff that no one in our society should have to endure. That's where anhedonia is quite useful, because I've just accepted whatever has happened as being normal and fine. At the same time, there has always been an underlying sense of injustice in my life.

Put it this way: if you never, ever have a positive experience in your life, and the whole world is full of people enjoying music, friends, weather, breathing etcetera, wouldn't you find it a bit unjust, unfair?

The difficult part is that I know what's funny, sad, enjoyable, boring. I know, most of the time, how I should react to things (which is what makes me such a great social chameleon). But I don't *feel* those reactions. It's like I have all the tinder and fuel for a fire, but nothing to create the spark.

I don't get enjoyment from anything, but I do get the let-downs that everyone else gets, because let-downs are practical, not emotional (losing a job, a car breaking down, the electric meter running out with no money to fill it). Without any enjoyment, ever, my life is nothing more than a series of problems that have to be solved. And that's it.

I'm always treading water, waiting for that next problem to come along, desperately trying to avoid that sense of injustice, yet experiencing it every day when I look at you and every other normal person.

That's how those more negative momentary flickers seep through, of disappointment, or frustration. When too many things go wrong all at once and I can't see a practical response to the situations I'm being faced with, I start to feel the injustice of everything – like my energy is being worn down – wondering how much more I can take, and as though I might not be able to cope. Like the time my girlfriend left me, my phone got cut off, my car was stolen and I lost my job all in one day. Disappointment flickered and then was gone, but I was left with a sense of injustice, and that if one more bad thing happened my head would go under water and that would be it, the pits of despair. I guess everyone probably experiences that, but, after a life full of knockdowns, and nothing positive, they might not be able to stop themselves 'going under'.

Half thankfully and half gloomily, I know that I can probably take anything that's ever thrown at me. I have so far. My lack of emotion has meant that instead of feeling sad, desperate or even suicidal at these times (and I have had more than my fair share of these times), I focus on finding a practical solution to the problem, and once I've decided on something I then move on. If there is no obvious solution – like when someone dies – I just shrug it off. Take the day my brother-in-law called to tell me my grandad had died. I said, 'Okay,' and got on with the washing up. It wasn't because I didn't like my grandad, but he was dead, what good would crying about it do? He wouldn't know. Death is part of life and life must go on. Next thing, please.

2

LIVING WITH SHIRLEY

Dr Greenberg: When eating a tasty food, do you ever try to eat it slowly, making it last longer?

Shirley Hughes, formerly Wells (and once, for not much more than a week when I was aged five or six, Cassidy) wasn't what you'd call 'motherly'. My first real memory of her, when I was around three years old, was walking into our kitchen to see her standing at the sink, holding a bin bag in the washing up water. I asked what she was doing – a quiet squeaking was coming from the bin bag – and she explained that she was drowning three kittens, because the owner didn't want them. That's what she did, to help our neighbours out and earn a few extra pounds.

Though we moved a few times when I was a baby, for much of my childhood we lived in a decent-sized, split-level council flat in Eccles, Manchester – Mum, Cath (my older sister) and me. For as long as I can remember, Shirley was never around.

And if she was, then I wasn't allowed to be. It was a rule that if she said I had to be out, I was out. I once spent five hours sat in heavy rain in the park, because I didn't have anywhere else to go, age four. Another afternoon, when it was boiling hot outside, I went home from playing on the estate because I was desperate for a drink and Mum caught me as I opened the flat door, yelling at me to get out. I told her that it was too hot outside and that I really needed a cup of water. Then a man I'd never seen before appeared, tall and with dark hair and a biker jacket. As Shirley told me to get out again, the man shoved me into the front door, crushing my hand between my shoulder and the white wood. He said I should listen to my mother and get out when I wasn't wanted. My hand ached for weeks after, until the school nurse told me she thought it was broken and sent me off to the hospital, where they strapped it up.

At night-times, when Shirley was out, I would lie in bed, listening to all the sounds of the estate around me, no money in the meter to put the lights on. It was a scary time in Manchester then, with Peter Sutcliffe on the loose across the North – a real life bogeyman, who'd killed real-life people not too far from where I lived. Everyone was talking about him and everyone was scared. If there was a creak from downstairs, a car backfiring outside, shouts from kicking out time at the local pub, I'd be convinced the 'Yorkshire Ripper' (or someone like him) was breaking into the flat, ready to kill my sister and me in our beds. I'd lie in the dark with the itchy, woollen blanket tucked tightly around me and, as loudly as I could, I'd shout, 'Dad, is that you? Back from boxing already?' naively hoping any intruder would get scared and run away.

I was a 'Latch Key Kid'. This meant I had my own key to get in and out of the flat because there was nobody home most of the time.

Thinking that Mum had anhedonia, some things make a bit more sense. For one, Shirley was always well turned out: a flowery dress, a short skirt, or flared trousers with a seam ironed neatly down the middle, and a smart jumper; her brown hair cropped around her ears, rolled in fluffy curls. My clothes generally didn't fit and were covered in holes and rips, and Shirley only cut my hair if we were due a visit with my grandparents. In fact, those were the only times I ever looked presentable. Those and photo days at school, so that a nice picture of Cath and me could be stuck on Nan's mantelpiece a few weeks later. For Nan and Grandad – the only other people in the world that might have cared about our upbringing – Shirley always put on a show, dressing us up and being all nice and friendly, like that's how we all normally were together. Cath and I played along, because that was what we did. We were brought up to think: 'that's just how life is', and had a get-on-with-it attitude. If you see photos of me as a child, you'll find a perfect smile slapped across my face. I was the king of smiling on cue. But notice the day-old haircut, the brand new clothes, fresh out the packet – knee-high socks, posh dungaree shorts, child-size suits, colourful shirts and tank tops – bought from the catalogue just for the occasion. As soon as we were home, or the visitors had gone, I was back into my ripped jeans and t-shirt, the new clothes taken away to be 'kept for best'. Shirley probably sent them back for a refund, because I never saw them again; by the time the next event came around that we needed 'best' clothes, we'd have outgrown the last ones anyway.

In those photos you'll notice a difference in build between us kids and our mother. As babies, Cath and I were both quite chubby, but as little kids that baby fat fell away leaving scrawny children who didn't eat a lot. Shirley, on the other hand, wasn't exactly what you'd call petite – not plump but definitely solid and well fed. It wasn't like I'd sit and watch her eating, saliva dripping from my mouth, more that she'd eat when I wasn't around, or while she was out, probably forgetting that Cath and I needed food as well.

If there were no tins of baked beans in the cupboard to scoff down while Shirley was out, I'd go through the kitchen bin to see what she might have thrown away, hoping for half a sandwich. When I was five, I woke up in the early hours one morning, starving for food because I hadn't eaten at all that day. I went downstairs and found Shirley at the kitchen table, eating a packet of biscuits. Though I was scared of what might happen – she was always irritable if I said I was hungry – I looked up to the ceiling and thought, *If there's a God there now, let my mum give me a biscuit…* then I took a big breath and asked her if I could please have one. Amazingly, she said yes and, as I took my biscuit back to my room, I remember thinking that there must be a God because her giving me food was such a rare thing.

The other indication that Shirley didn't care about me should have been the amount of money she had lying around, but I never questioned it. I always knew we were poor – because of how I was dressed, and because just about everyone in our area was – but Shirley's tin in the upper right kitchen cupboard always had a big stash of ten pound and twenty pound notes in it. I was about seven years old when I first started climbing on a chair to swipe a note from that tin, thinking she'd never miss it, but somehow she always knew. And whenever she found me out, the belt would appear and she'd thrash me with the buckle end.

Her beatings started when I was just a toddler, always for bad behaviour of some sort: I wasn't an easy child. I'd do something wrong and she'd shout a lot then take off her belt, whipping the buckle around; when it caught me, it stung. I'd try to avoid it, ducking out of the way, but that would just make her madder. She didn't care where she hit – in those days, the teachers never bothered if you were covered in cuts and bruises, not like now – and I'd end up with small gashes across my face. I'd hold my hands up, trying to protect my eyes and the buckle would slash into my bare arms instead, leaving a series of perfectly straight, bloody lines in my skin.

One weekend, not long before I turned seven, my nan and grandad were due to visit and so Shirley made us some porridge for breakfast. Because I was in the routine of not eating much – especially not in the morning – I really didn't want it, no matter how many times she told me to eat. I meant to slide it across the table, just a bit away from me, but I pushed too hard and the next thing I knew the bowl had flown straight across the table, into the wall and down to the floor below, porridge and pieces of china going everywhere.

Shirley's glare moved from the bowl to me. She grabbed both my shoulders, her short nails digging in through my t-shirt, and wrenched me up from my chair. All I could think was: my nan and grandad are coming, there's no way she's going to hit me. But I was wrong.

She pulled me along the hallway, up the stairs, banging my head repeatedly against the wall. As we got into my room she yanked off one of her blue Scholl sandals and, holding the heel, she started smacking me round the head with the hard wooden sole, over and over again.

'Don't!' I shouted. 'Me nan's coming, me nan's coming!'

I thought that would stop her, make her see she was going too far. But she carried on. I tried to put my hands up, but they stung with the slap of the sandal, and I crumbled to the floor.

Then she was on top of me, pinning me down, my arms stuck by my sides, pulling her belt from round her trousers and smacking my chest and face with the buckle. I tried my hardest to make tears come to my eyes and cried out, hoping that if she saw me cry she'd stop. Eventually I managed my goal, forced tears rolling down my cheeks, and she got off me. I quickly moved across the thin carpet, away from her, running my hands over my head, feeling the bumps already coming up through my scraggly hair.

She stood in the doorway, breathing heavily, then turned and left.

When my nan and grandad arrived, I heard her tell them I'd been really naughty and wasn't allowed down for the rest of the day. I sat in my room waiting it out; not feeling sorry for myself, just waiting until the moment I'd be allowed out of the flat.

The beatings happened for all sorts of reasons at all sorts of times, generally because I was cheeky and not respecting her. She'd ask me to do something – like take my school bag to my room – and I'd always have a reason not to. And that would lead to another beating. Sometimes she'd forcibly take my snake belt off me, to add to the indignity, wrapping the blue and white elastic round her hand and going at me with the thin S-shaped buckle that stung worse than her normal belt.

To avoid Mum's punishments – and also because she told me to 'get out' basically every time she saw me – I spent a lot of time outside. In the daytime, especially if it was raining, I'd go down to Linda and Margaret's flat, on the landing below ours.

They were strawberry-blonde sisters from the most well-to-do family I knew: always dressed more primly than everyone else on our estate, and Celia, the girls' mum, had nice china figurines and lace doilies all over their flat. Linda and Margaret were Cath's friends first, but I didn't mind being around Margaret. I've always been what a psychotherapist would describe as 'a rescuer' – basically, though I don't see females as being weak, or even needing protection, I still tend to take a protective role towards them, instinctively. It's that relationship that I had with Margaret as kids. She was the younger sister, getting left out of Linda and Cath's games, so I'd sit on the soft carpet of her bedroom floor listening to her chat away to me, playing with her dolls as she did, talking about all sorts and telling me stories.

The girls had strict bedtimes though, and

preferring to be doing something than to sit pointlessly doing nothing in my flat alone at night, I searched elsewhere for entertainment in the evenings. I made friends with a group on the estate whose parents didn't care if they were out late either – though no parent seemed to care as little as mine – and we'd hang around getting ourselves into trouble. It was one of the estate kids, Mark Burgess, who showed me how different my family situation was from everyone else's. He was a foster kid whose parents had both died when he was little and, one day, in a sad, almost despairing voice, he told me: 'I'm glad I met you, I'm not as bad off as you are.' I asked him how he could even think this, his parents had died! He said, "I would rather dead parents that loved me than live parents who didn't want to know me. This orphan felt sorry for me. Not that I cared, but I kind of saw what he meant: I never understood why Shirley bothered to have children in the first place. She seemed so uninterested in having us around, but it's not like we were accidents, I always thought that I must remind her of my dad.

Shirley got married when she was twenty-one to my dad, David Hughes, who was in the army. His work meant they travelled around a bit and I was born in a British military hospital in Hanover, West Germany. But when we moved back to England – first to Leeds, then to the Manchester area – with me less than a year old, my father didn't come with us. According to my Auntie Mags, they split because Shirley had 'male visitors' over to the house when he was at work. I can see why that didn't go down well with a man who, after leaving the army, became a wandering preacher.

I can't say I'm bitter towards my dad for leaving us, because that would require some kind of interest in him to begin with. The only reason I've met him as an adult – around ten years ago – was because my sister had wanted to find him. As a father myself now, I can see that he should have been there to protect me from Shirley's abuse and neglect, but he wasn't and that's just the way it is. How would being bitter about it all change the past?

Anyway, I think I either reminded Mum of our dad, or she blamed me for him leaving us; she certainly never laid into Cath in the way she did me, at least, not as far as I know. My sister was treated quite differently from me, and though she may not have had an idyllic childhood, she was, in my mind, the golden girl. At Christmas, Mum would have a couple of presents for Cath, but would tell me to 'get out' like she did every other day. I'd wander round the estate, maybe knock on a few of my mates' doors to see if any of them could come out, not that they ever could. Instead of wishing for presents for myself – right from the go, I never believed in Santa (and I thought anyone who did was an absolute baby) – I'd just be hoping one of my friends had gotten a bike as their present so that there'd be someone I could hang around with for a while. I didn't mind not getting Christmas gifts when my sister did because I didn't covet anything, right from that very young age. I just saw Cath as being the favourite and that was that. In retrospect, the holes in my sister's clothes were just as bad as mine and she never got fed square meals either. Like me, she was never at home, so her relationship with Shirley can't have been that dissimilar to mine.

The only thing Mum ever showed a vague interest in, other than occasionally Cath, was her cat, Charlie. I have no idea where he came from, but this little white tabby would sit on Mum's lap and purr while she stroked it and watched episodes of *Starsky and Hutch*. You can probably picture some Hollywood movie with a sad child standing out in the cold, envious of the misplaced love the cat was getting, but that wasn't my reality. As with everything else, I really didn't mind that the cat got more attention than I did. I don't think I even noticed at the time. Obviously, I didn't like being hit with a wooden sandal, or taking a beating from the belt, but other than that, Shirley's neglectful parenting really didn't bother me. It never even struck me as wrong or odd. I had my independence and that suited me. That was the life I was used to, it's only now I have children of my own that I can see how things weren't right.

It's strange, but I don't remember my sister being around in our childhood, not after being tiny toddlers together, and she doesn't remember me in hers, either. Neither of us spent time in the flat – I guess she had to find her own friends in order to survive too – and from the age of three I was independent, fending for myself. I kept out of the flat all day, took myself off on the mile-and-a-half walk to nursery school, and had to find my own food. The dinner ladies used to remark on my appetite, saying, 'Where are you putting it all?' and laughing along as I went back for bowl after bowl of savoury rice with sultanas. They had no idea that I felt I had to stock up on food whenever it was available to me.

If I got beaten up by bigger kids on the estate, or

on my way to school – something that happened a lot, the kids on the estate and in the wider area all knew that nobody was looking after me, so I was fair game – Shirley never commented that my bag or clothes were ripped, and she didn't mention any new cuts and bruises I might have on my arms, legs and face. If she did notice, she probably assumed they were from her own hand. Besides, we barely spent any time together, so she never got the chance to see new scars. We only sat down at the same time if visitors were coming round.

3

VISITING TIME, AGE FIVE

Dr Greenberg: *Does it make you feel good when someone you care about reaches out to touch you?*

'Your nan and grandad are coming tomorrow,' Shirley said to me when we crossed at the front door.

It was eight on a Friday night in early autumn. I was five.

I was just coming in, my mates all gone home for the night. Shirley was just going out.

'Make sure you're up early.' The door slammed shut behind her.

And so, on Saturday morning, I dragged myself out of bed as soon as I woke up and went straight through to the kitchen. Shirley was sitting at the table, a mug of something hot between her hands.

'Sit down,' she said.

I took a deep breath and pulled out a chair. Mum

winced as the metal legs scraped across the floor.

'You're a state,' she said.

Shirley stood up and came round the table. She was wearing a black dress with big pink flowers all over it that I hadn't seen before, and a bright white cardigan on top.

These were her clothes for visitors, all posh and neatly pressed, and I knew she'd have got me something new to wear as well.

She stood right behind me, her perfume filling my nose with its sickly floweriness.

'What you doing?' I said, turning my head up to her.

The hair scissors were clutched in one of her hands. She knocked the side of my head with her other hand, forcing me to look straight ahead.

'Sit still.'

This was the routine: haircut, wash, new clothes, wait. But that didn't mean I wanted it to happen.

'My hair's fine, it doesn't need it.'

'I said, sit still.'

'I am.'

She clipped me round the ear and I shut up.

I watched inch-long strands of hair fall onto my arm and down to the floor. She snipped away for ages, then turned me round to face her. As she cut above my eyes I held my breath as tight as I could, in case I annoyed her by breathing too much and she started rowing with me. But she didn't even seem to notice me, just concentrated hard on what she was doing, getting a perfectly straight edge across my eyebrows.

Cath strolled into the room wearing pyjamas that were clearly too small for her, much like my own. She sat down at the table across from me.

'Get yourself some cereal,' Shirley said to her.

Cath slid off her seat and started rummaging through the cupboard for a bowl.

Another clip round the side of my head and Mum told me she was done.

'Sink,' she said. I opened my mouth to tell her I was clean enough, that I didn't need a wash, but she held up a finger to silence me. 'Now.'

I peeled myself out of my pyjamas and stood there, shivering, while Shirley dragged the chair across the room for me to stand on. She flicked on the hot tap.

'Up.'

I was used to these one-word instructions from her. They saved time and got everything over and done with as quickly as possible. But I hated getting onto the work surface naked and washing in the sink, in case all my mates were in the field below. They'd see me starkers and I'd never live it down. It was bad enough doing it in front of Cath, though she was concentrating on pouring milk onto her *Special K*, and not even looking at me.

I climbed up and peered out. No one seemed to be around. Quick as I could, I started the washing routine. Face. Arms. Bits. Legs. Back of the neck and behind the ears. Feet. The water was boiling hot, but I didn't care: it was better than too cold. And Shirley watched me the whole while, making sure I got myself clean enough.

As soon as I'd finished my last little toe, she snapped her next order at me: 'Go and get dressed, there's clothes on my bed. And be quick.'

She turned to Cath and I jumped off the worktop and ran straight upstairs.

I wasn't usually allowed in Shirley's bedroom and opening the door seemed wrong, even though I'd got permission. Two neatly folded piles of clothes lay on the yellow sheet, fresh out of the brown postage packet that sat next to them. One pile had a pink dress on top; the other some sort of mustard-coloured t-shirt. I grabbed that one and ran through to my room, still naked, dropped it on the bed and quickly inspected what she'd got me. It wasn't too bad: a dark yellow t-shirt with a fancy button-up collar and a black band around its lower half, and dark blue trousers that had a seam pressed straight down the front like some kind of Navy uniform. These were better than the last clothes she'd got me for a visit to Nan and Grandad's in the spring. Then, I'd had to wear a pair of short dungarees and long socks that almost reached my knees and seemed like something Linda and Margaret would wear. Shirley might have even borrowed them from Celia for all I knew. I hurried to get into the new, starchy clothes, the fabrics immediately itching around my freshly scrubbed skin. I glanced down and saw lines from where the trousers had been folded in the post still in the legs, and my t-shirt was creased in a cross over my chest.

'What's taking so long?' Mum called from downstairs.

'Nothing,' I shouted back.

'Then get down here.'

The haircut, wash and clothes were just the start. Now we had to get lunch ready and watch Mum agitatedly pacing between the rooms, checking at the living room window every two minutes to see if Grandad's car was pulling onto the estate.

I went back downstairs to the kitchen. Cath was sweeping up a mound of hair from the floor. She'd been hacked at too; it looked as though Shirley had stuck a bowl over her head and trimmed round the edge, blunt cuts making it all stick out at angles on the top. But I knew better than to laugh at her.

'Michael!' Shirley shouted from the living room.

I wandered through. Sure enough, there Shirley was, leaning over the sofa, her hand up against the window, her pointy nose almost touching the glass. She twisted round as I entered, inspecting me from a distance. 'You'll do,' she said. And she turned back to the window, craning her head up and down to get a better view.

She was always on edge on visitor days. She wanted everything to seem normal in her parents' eyes. She would put on a massive spread, with a hot dinner and then cold meats for tea. I think I assumed she was putting herself in debt with all the expense just to make out that she was doing well, to her parents. Kind of for their benefit.

Which is why she had Cath and me all dressed up and out of our ripped jeans and t-shirts. I thought she didn't want them to know how poor we actually were.

I know now that she could easily afford it all. And pleasing them wasn't the motive for her show: for some unknown reason, she didn't want them to take us away from her.

'Don't just stand there, then,' Shirley said. 'Come and help.'

I had no idea why she wanted me to help her keep lookout, she never usually did.

'What do you want me to do?'

'Get over here. I can't see a bloody thing.' She gestured out the window. 'Fucking scaffold's in the way.'

Scaffolding had been cladding our block for the last couple of months, while the council did some work on the roof. They seemed to have finished it ages ago and just left the scaffold up.

'How am I supposed to know if they've got here or not?' she continued. 'You need to get out there and move those boards for me.'

I climbed onto the sofa next to her and looked out at the scaffolding.

'Get those trousers rolled up over your knees,' she said, 'so you don't ruin them.'

I did as I was told while Shirley unlatched the window and pushed, holding it as wide as it went so I could climb over the back of the sofa and out.

'Off you go,' she said.

There was a gap of about half a foot from the window to the scaffolding. This was definitely something to tell the lads at school: guess what Mum let me do at the weekend?

I squeezed myself onto the window ledge and carefully put one leg across the gap, then the other. The wood of the board spiked into my bare knees and palms as I pulled myself fully out. It was weird being so high above the ground with nothing there to protect me.

'Move that one–' Shirley, her arm sticking as far out the window as she could get it, pointed to the third board away from the flat '–and let's see if the gap's big enough.'

I hesitated, considering how far down it was to the ground – basically a drop of seven floors. Shirley had let the window slip shut and was shouting something about fruit at Cath, who must have still been in the kitchen. I could see for miles from here, more so than when I was inside the flat, and I wondered why Shirley didn't just come out herself, if it was so important to her to see them coming.

'What are you waiting for?' Shirley said from behind me, her attention fully back on my task again.

I didn't need telling twice. I shuffled onto the board next to me, a large splinter wedging itself in the fleshy bit of my left palm as I went. My stubby fingers barely reached around the thickness of the board and I pulled at it with everything I had. But it was around eight feet long and really heavy; it rose only about an inch before my fingers slipped off the edge and it thudded back into its original position.

'I can't do it, Mum.'

'Oh, for fuck's sake.' Her cheeks started to colour and her eyes narrowed. I knew exactly what that meant and I didn't want another beating.

'Sorry, I'll try again.'

I leaned over and wedged my fingers in, trying to grasp the board and pull at the same time, but it wasn't working and I sat back, stretching my aching fingers.

'Are you going to sit there all day or actually move the things?'

I tried again, but this time I pushed my hands between the two boards. The one I was trying to move shunted over so I could fit my hands right in and under the bottom of the plank. I pulled and pulled and pulled, until, in a quick movement, I managed to force the board upwards. The drop through to the ground opened up and I was staring straight down, past Margaret and Linda's landing to the paving and grass below. I wished they would come out right then and glance up, see me out on the scaffolding. But no one was around. With all my strength I leant forward and kind of folded the plank over, so it banged down onto the one behind it, not far from the edge.

I turned to Mum but she didn't meet my eyes. Instead, she was craning her neck to see out through the gap I'd made.

'That'll do, I suppose. Now, get back in here.'

'Can't I just sit here and watch out for you? I can see for miles. I'll concentrate really hard and shout you as soon as I see Grandad's car.'

'Of course you can't. How would that look to your nan and grandad if you're out there when they pull up?'

She stuck out her arm to help me in. I steadied myself on her, the wool of her cardigan soft under my sore fingers, and climbed onto the windowsill, back into the flat.

The living room felt strangely warm as I clambered off the windowsill and over the back of the sofa. A smell of pastry melting in the oven came from the kitchen.

Shirley tore herself away from the window a moment to check me over. 'Look at the state of you, get yourself sorted out.'

It was like she'd totally forgotten that I'd just helped her. I stood there, knowing not to say a word, but not sure what she was expecting of me.

'Well,' she said, like it was obvious. She turned back to the window and gazed out of her new viewing point.

I went back through to the kitchen and found Cath at the table, mixing something in a big china bowl.

She glanced up at me, then returned to her mixing. 'You're all dusty. Go and brush yourself off and roll your trousers back down.'

'What's that?' I asked her, pointing to the bowl.

'Cream for the fruit salad.'

*

The council had scaffolding up on our block a lot of the time when I was a kid. Always fixing gutters, or painting windows, or replacing tiles, or whatever. Shifting the boards for Shirley to see more easily became part of the routine when Nan and Grandad were coming to ours on one of the twice-yearly visits, right up until I was about ten years old: haircut, wash, shift the scaffold boards, new clothes.

From the moment Grandad's Mark III Escort pulled onto the estate, operations were conducted with military precision.

Nan and Grandad would knock on the flat door, Shirley would answer while Cath and I stood back, our hands clasped neatly in front of us, watching our manners.

They'd come in and it would be hugs all round.

My grandparents weren't bad to be around, so I didn't mind playing the game of being nice for them, but hugging people has never done anything for me and it always felt strangely awkward. Shirley would bring tea into the lounge and we'd all sit there, the grown-ups talking, Cath and I sitting nicely on the floor, being seen and not heard.

A timer would ping in the kitchen, and Shirley would hurry through, opening the oven and filling the flat with the smell of meat and gravy.

'Dinner,' she'd call, in her dull tones – not like Nan's sing-song voice – and we'd all file through to the kitchen, all with huge appetites and delighted that she'd cooked such a delicious meal.

We'd eat pie with vegetables and potatoes and gravy, the grown-ups would talk and I would watch my manners.

After, Grandad would take me out for a kick about with a new ball he'd brought me. Then 'the women', as he called them, would come down and we'd be forced to pose for photographs together.

Mum would smooth out my hair and pouf up Cath's sleeves and Nan would tell us to say 'cheese' just before the blinding flash went off. Sometimes Shirley would stand with us, clutching one of us to each side of her, other times it would just be Cath and me, hand in hand or in an awkward hug, but always all of us would be smiling our faces off.

Then it would be teatime. The cold meats and salad would come out, chopped up bits of cucumber and tomato and carrot, some fresh bread, maybe a few hard-boiled eggs. The grown-ups would talk and I'd watch my manners.

Soon after, Grandad would say: 'Right, we best be off then. Long drive ahead.' And he and Nan would kiss us all goodbye and tell us how well we looked and then go out to their car. Mum would watch them pull off, then she'd nip up to her bedroom, get changed and be out the front door in less than five minutes. Visiting hours well and truly over.

4

THE NETWORK

Dr Greenberg: Do you feel close to your friends?

Survival for me as a kid meant using my friends as a kind of rotating network to get food and clean clothes. I'd hang around my friends' houses at teatime, hoping one of their mums would ask me to stay. Margaret and Linda's mum, Celia, always had an extra plate for me. But other mums had to watch their budgets and couldn't keep feeding another mouth, so only sometimes asked me to stay. Many of the kids on the estate – Daniel Wright, Eric, Adam and Chris Kirby, Marie Piechota – were in almost as poor a state as I was. But, though their parents generally struggled to keep them with the meagre benefits they received, they always had food in their kitchen cupboards. Unlike Shirley, who had a tin full of money but no food to feed us.

When I started at Moorfield County Primary proper, I extended my network to the kids who lived near the school. For one thing, some bigger kids had decided that regularly beating me up was fair game – I had no one at home looking out for me who'd go and tell their parents – so I had to avoid them as much as I could. Gary Michaels, a lad of about sixteen, lived on our landing and every time I walked past his front door in the morning to get to the flat stairwell, he'd grab me by the neck of my jumper and give me a good punch in the face, just for a laugh. To avoid him, I'd climb over the railings outside our flat, slide down the supporting bar and swing onto Linda and Margaret's landing. Once I was free from him, I then had the ginger twins who lived down Addison Road to deal with. They were older than me too and they'd wait for me in the ginnels between the houses, completely out of sight. If they spotted me coming, they'd jump out just as I approached and beat me up, kicking and punching me, ripping my clothes and leaving me with scrapes on my arms.

I'd leave the flat early just to avoid these encounters, and would usually end up at Phillip Dean's house, virtually next to the school. Phillip had a rare skin condition and was wrinkled from head to foot. I wouldn't say I liked him – there's no one I've ever actually liked or disliked– but I didn't mind hanging around at his. He lived just round the corner from the school and Mrs Dean took a bit of a shine to me, giving me tea and toast every single morning. After school, I'd hang around with Pete Richards or Darren Black – the hardest kids in my year – before going back to the estate. Pete might stick some beans on for me, if he was eating while I was there. And if Darren was putting a load of washing on (he was a resourceful kid) he'd throw in my grimy jeans and t-shirt too. I'd sit around in me grundies – providing I was wearing some that day – until it was all washed and dried, or I'd pinch something of Darren's to wear. Darren would try and persuade his mum to let me have tea with them too, but if Mrs Black said that it was time for me to leave – code for, 'I'm not feeding him again tonight' – I'd go over to the estate to see if there was another option. Mrs Kirby would often let me stay for tea at theirs, and Mrs Piechota too. If none of them invited me to stay, I'd never ask to join, or say that I was hungry: I didn't want to be labelled a scrounger, even to this day I never ask for help. Instead, I'd go without.

On the weekends, I might go and see Darren and we'd head round the Conny Club, a few doors down from his house and the place where his dad could always be found.

We'd ask for 50p to buy some sweets or something, but would end up staying there, sitting under the table, his dad passing his lager down to us every so often for a cheeky swig.

On the off chance I'd go to a market on the weekend with Marie and her mum, or Celia and the girls, someone would always buy an extra t-shirt or pair of shorts off the rack for me to have. It was this kind of generosity that saw me through childhood. I never cared what they might think of me, whether they pitied and felt sorry for me, I just knew what I needed to survive.

Don't get me wrong, these families weren't pictures of domestic bliss either. Darren's mum and dad were together, but his dad was never home, always drinking down the Conny Club. I never saw Pete's parents, though he had several older brothers who were generally kicking around his house and making sure he was okay.

Marie's parents obviously cared about her, but they were always going out and leaving her home alone. And the same with Adam, Chris and Eric's parents, who stayed out drinking all night. So, as seven- and eight-year-olds, we'd all be out together until two or three in the morning, no one caring where we were.

The majority of the kids I hung around with were tearaways. Although I take full responsibility for my actions throughout my life, these were the kids who got me into trouble, because I always agreed to go along with anything that was suggested, not ever considering the repercussions, for me or anyone else. It was far easier to say 'yes' to something than to say 'no', because saying 'no' meant questions would be asked, and questions meant that turmoil in my head about why I didn't know if I should do something or not. What I now know as anhedonia. It was too hard to explain to another lad, especially when they got a kick out of whatever trouble it was, and I didn't. So 'yes' was the simplest answer to any suggestion that was thrown my way.

If I met up with Pete and Darren before school, we wouldn't go in. Instead, we'd walk to the farmer's fields near Barton Airport and make dens, or climb the electricity pylons, building ourselves rope swings from the bars and daring each other to jump from silly heights. Or we'd wander into town and loiter near the shops, pushing one another in front of passing cars as we went. There was one shop that used to keep its bottles of pop at the entrance, so we'd quickly open the front door and whip one out, without the shopkeeper seeing. Then, after we'd drunk it, we'd have the cheek to take the bottle back in the shop and claim our 10p for returning the glass. Now and again we'd go and sit with the Rastafarians in a café Pete knew. They'd be smoking cannabis and would tell us about how it was a way of life for them, that they kept a level high by smoking in moderation. The greedy English, they said, smoked it all wrong, having virtual 'pot parties', as they called them. If the Rastas got talking about smack-heads we'd be there for ages; they despised them like there was nothing more disgusting on the earth. Sometimes, we'd go round the old houses near the school, daring each other to smash a window, or knocking the ends off the old gas meters and stealing all the 50p pieces from inside to buy ourselves sweets or football cards. Most days, we'd go to Kingsy's shop, where the owner – a balding bloke with leathery, tanned skin – kept a box of 1p cigarettes on the counter, next to a box of halfpenny matches. If you told him you didn't have enough for a match as well as a cigarette, he'd lean over the counter and, with a small lighter clutched in his big, meaty hands, he'd light it for you. When I first tried cigarettes, like any kid new to smoking I puffed the smoke in and blew it straight back out again. But Pete laughed at me and told me I was embarrassing him. 'You're doing it wrong,' he said. 'You're supposed to breathe it in.' And, just like that, at age eight, I learnt to smoke the right way.

In school, we were just as unruly, though I never saw anything I did as being that wrong. I was just mimicking my mates, going along with the things they did because it was easier to say 'yes' than 'no'. We'd impersonate the teachers and get into trouble. We'd chat about what we were doing that night, or come the weekend, and the teacher would tell us to shut up. We'd answer back, laugh at each other, throw paper aeroplanes and spit balls. In break times, we'd chuck rocks over the fence, aiming for the Catholic school kids next door. Basically, we were just being boys. But all our boyish behaviour meant that every single Friday morning we were forced to queue up outside the headmaster's office, waiting for six of the best. The cane or the slipper – which was actually a trainer – across the backside, or the edge of a ruler across the knuckles. That one stung.

The worst part of being sent for the cane was standing in the queue, waiting for your turn to come. The actual caning part wasn't that bad, it was the anticipation that was the killer. From inside Mr Granger's office there'd be a sharp thwack then a muffled cry, another thwack and a stronger cry, and this would go on and on, boy after boy until it got to your turn. Darren, Pete and I were all the usual suspects in that queue, there each week without fail, and we knew the drill. We took great pleasure in watching the first-timers virtually wetting themselves, shivering and shaking while they waited for their turn. None of us ever shed a tear when Mr Granger got going on us; we wouldn't be caught dead crying in school. So whenever a little kid came out in tears we'd all fall over each other laughing and calling them cry-babies, asking if they wanted their mummies. Even then, I didn't find things funny like the other lads did, but I needed them to accept me as one of them, so I'd laugh just as hard.

Mr Granger wasn't that vicious, and he didn't

linger over the punishments like he was enjoying himself, taking pleasure in our pain. He just got on with it: 'Right, skipping school again, was it?' he'd say. 'Bend over.' I didn't even resent him for the lashings, knowing he was just doing his job and appreciating his quick efficiency.

Primary school was a good time for me. I was almost entirely supported by the network, I got fed really well because school dinners were funded, and I had people to hang out with so I didn't have a reason to go home. It became normal that I'd just go back to the flat to sleep, and sometimes to pinch a bit of cash from Shirley's tin.

It was also normal that I'd keep a watch out for other kids that might become my friends and therefore useful to me. So when I was on my own one teatime after school, hanging around waiting for Daniel or Adam to come out of theirs, and a kid I'd never seen before approached me and asked me if I wanted to come over to his, I said yes.

I think he said his name was Kenny. He had a Manchester accent, same as me, and was wearing clothes that weren't any better than mine. His green t-shirt was faded down the front, like he'd been lying out in the sun for days.

He climbed up on the wall I was sitting on and kicked it with his heels like I was.

'You live here?' he said.

'Yeah. Up there.' I pointed to my block. 'You new?'

'Yeah,' he said. 'Why aren't you in for your tea, it's teatime isn't it?'

'Why aren't you?' I said, avoiding such a dumb question.

'Do you want to come to mine to see what Dad's cooking?'

'Your dad does the cooking?' I said. None of my other friends' dads did the cooking.

'Sure. Come on.' He leapt off the wall and started running over to the flat block across from mine.

I jumped down and followed him.

5

DO YOU LIKE BOATS?

Dr Greenberg: Do your emotional responses seem very different from those of other people?

I didn't know anyone in this block, so had never been inside, even though I'd lived opposite it for five years. It turned out to be just like ours. The stairs were solid concrete, the railings were metal, and a weird smell came from one of the landings we passed. Like stale curry mixed with piss. Four floors up and Kenny turned along the landing.

'This way,' he called back to me. Then he disappeared through an open flat door.

I walked along the landing, gazing over at my block, level with our flat. There was no sign of Shirley or Cath inside.

Kenny's flat was dark, the corridor ahead lit up only from the door behind me. I squinted and realised there were thin brown sheets covering the windows in the lounge ahead. I couldn't see Kenny, but some man was sitting on the arm of a sofa.

'Come on in, lad,' the guy said, beckoning with his hand, prompting me to move into the lounge.

Kenny was standing in the centre of the room. It was strangely furnished, just a round dinner table against one wall, two pale cord armchairs and matching sofa, and a dog cage in the far corner. A thin, middle-aged man with flecked hair was sitting on one side of the sofa, his skin pale and grey, making him look ill. A hippy-looking woman in a floaty top and flares stood beside him, and a third man was slumped in the far armchair, his fat gut making his checked shirt bulge out and a thin blond comb-over covering his head. Behind the woman and the empty armchair, a map covered almost the whole of one wall. Little pins stuck out of it, like it was something from a wartime movie.

'Alright?' I said, wondering why everyone was staring at me.

The guy who'd told me to come in got up; he was tall and about the same age as my mum. He gently shut the lounge door, then turned to face me, running a hand through his thick black hair. 'Let's get this going, then,' he said, nodding past me at Kenny.

I turned. Kenny just stood there awkwardly, picking at a loose bit of thread on the hem of his t-shirt, yet still watching the man.

'Go on, hit him!' the man said.

'What?' A hundred thoughts ran through my head, mostly wondering why a grown-up man was asking this boy I'd never met to hit me.

'Hit him,' he said again, more forcefully, when Kenny still didn't move.

'Yeah, come on, hit him,' the thin man on the sofa joined in, his voice gravelly like he'd been smoking too much.

The lad still didn't move.

'I'm not fighting anyone,' I said, trying to sound brave, and I turned to leave.

'You're not going anywhere,' the main guy said. His voice was cool and he moved forward to block my path. 'If you're not going to fight, get your clothes off.'

I froze on the spot, confused about the situation, about why he was asking me to get undressed and why the woman wasn't telling the man to stop teasing me – like my friends' mums always did when someone took a joke too far. I knew I didn't get things in the same way that other people did, but even to me this seemed strange and unsettling.

'He told you to strip.' This came from the guy in the armchair. He levered himself up, his gut tightening out as he stood, showing him to be a solid block. He held up a spiked, two-prong fork, the kind you'd use to carve up a roast chicken, and jabbed it at me. 'Get your clothes off, now.'

I glanced at Kenny, but he was watching the floor, the thread of his t-shirt still clutched in his hand. This guy was deadly serious and not messing around. I stripped down to my pants, leaving my clothes in a pile between mine and Kenny's feet.

'Those too,' the man with the comb-over said, jabbing my grundies with the fork, hard, enough to leave a bruise.

I let them to the floor and stood there, stark bollock naked. All three men and the woman watching me. I had no idea what else to do: I was outnumbered and outsized. The main guy nodded at the woman, then grabbed my pile of clothes and bundled them up, chucking them into the gap between the sofa and the wall.

'Do you like boats?' the woman asked suddenly. She stepped over to me and put a hand on my shoulder, her warm fingers wrapping round my cold skin.

'I dunno,' I said.

'Have you ever been on a boat?' she said, and flicked her long hair behind one ear like she was flirting. But the pressure of her hand on my shoulder increased and I moved in the direction she was guiding me.

'No,' I said.

The main guy opened a little mesh door in the cage in the corner of the room. Now I was closer to it, I could see there were no soft blankets in the bottom, or dog chews, and no water bowl; no sign of a pet dog.

'In you go,' the main guy said, swinging his arm between me and the cage, like he was gesturing for me to board the boat the woman had been on about.

'I'm not getting in there,' I said.

I heard the door of the lounge open, and as I turned my head, I saw Kenny slip out the room with the man from the sofa close behind him.

The big guy with the fork prodded me again and I jumped forward as the prongs stung my arse cheek.

'Just get in,' he said. And jabbed me once more.

My backside throbbed. I got down on all fours and crawled through the small gap into the cage, the thin bars of metal sending sharp pains into my bony knees. I pretty much filled the thing, my head pushing against the top and only a little room in front and behind me. I reckoned I could barely turn round.

The big guy put down his prodding fork and pulled a padlock from his trouser pocket, then crouched in front of me, fastening the lock on the cage, his thin blond hair flopping forward as he moved. Very deliberately, so I could see, he held up the key and slipped it into his checked shirt pocket.

'Come on,' the main guy said to the woman, and they crossed the room to the table and started going through some papers.

The big guy sat in the armchair beside the cage, twisting his fork in his hands. 'So, do you like boats, or not?' he asked, grinning down at me, his teeth all yellowed.

I shrugged, still completely confused by this cage and why the hell they were asking about boats to a boy who lived on a council estate in Manchester. We weren't by the sea, so how would I ever have even seen a boat in real life?

'Don't just shrug, answer me,' he said. 'Do you like them?'

'I don't know,' I said. It was an honest answer: I didn't know.

The lounge door opened and the third man came back in, Kenny now not with him.

He moved straight to the map on the wall and started examining a section of it.

'The larger the boat,' continued the big guy, still smirking at me, 'the better. You know why?' He raised his eyebrows, like he was about to reveal a big secret or something. 'Less seasickness on the big ones. And that's a fact. Did you know that?'

'No.'

'So, knowing that, if you were to go on a boat, you'd probably want a big one, right?'

'I guess.'

'You guess! Bit vacant, aren't you? Come on, give me some commitment: do you want to go on a boat? Does it excite you, the open sea?'

'Maybe. I don't know.' The man's eyes narrowed and I could see he wanted me to agree with him. 'Yes.'

He grinned and got up from his chair, then bent down to me in the cage. I was still on all fours, my head touching the top, the bars digging into my knees.

'There's a good lad,' he said. His breath was stale on my face. Then he raised the fork and jabbed my shoulder before I could move back. 'You just stay there, and keep being good.'

For the next couple of hours, the men and the woman paced the room, talking between each other, shuffling through papers, scanning the map on the wall.

I studied my surroundings wondering how the hell I'd get out. There was nothing in the room except the sparse furniture. There wasn't even a phone to call for help. Though there was a door across from the window, probably leading onto the kitchen like it did in my flat. Not that it was much help if I couldn't get to it. All I could see was an ashtray on the floor beside the sofa that I might be able to use to hit one of them at some point. Not a lot of good against five adults, and I couldn't reach it anyway. There was nothing else to use as a weapon if they ever did let me out. It was such a weird room, with that map on the wall and the brown sheets covering the window. The whole place stank of tarry cigarettes, but if I was going to be spending a long time in this cage, I was just pleased there weren't blood stains up the walls and shit trodden into the carpet. I wrapped my arms around my legs, trying to keep in my body warmth, and sat quietly, waiting for something to happen. But nothing did.

When it got dark outside, they left.

I tried curling up in the cage, hunched up in the bottom of it, and I slept on and off throughout the night, waking up every so often with cramping pains running through my limbs, trying to stretch myself out of the stiffness, then attempting to get back to sleep.

In the morning, around what must have been eight or nine, the group of adults returned, another couple of men with them. The big guy with the blond comb-over sat in his chair next to me and produced his prodding fork, jamming it into my thigh and grinning broadly.

'Don't,' I said. 'I'm dying for a pee.' He chuckled and jabbed at me again.

'Don't let him piss everywhere,' the main guy from the day before said. His arm was wrapped around the woman's shoulders as they stood at the table once again.

'You best come with me then, lad,' the big man said. He stepped round the cage and unlocked the padlock, letting the door swing open.

I crawled out, my body stiff and aching with every movement. I stretched as I got to my feet, letting my muscles realign.

'Bet that feels good, lad?' the big guy said.

I gave half a smile, like he expected me to, but of course it didn't feel good. Then he clasped me by the wrist and out we went into the hallway. The toilet was just like ours, a little room next to the front door with only a tiny window. Nothing in there but the loo and one yellow bog roll.

'No fucking around. And be quick,' he said.

I went inside and wondered whether I could get the window open. But he left the door open a few inches, his hand wedged firmly round it to stop me slamming it shut, and I decided there was no way I was getting out without him hearing. I peed and went back to him.

*

This is how it went for the next forty-eight hours. They brought me cups of water every so often, and I'd ask to go to the toilet once I got desperate. They talked and talked about God knows what, sorting through papers and referring to their map over and over, moving the pins around and arguing with each other about where things were. Once in a while the big guy would come and sit in his chair next to me and prod me with his fork, taunting me and telling me boating facts, as though I cared. But, mostly, they all ignored me, like I wasn't even there. As soon as it got dark out, they all left, and I was alone in the empty, silent flat. I tried shouting out a couple of times, but no one heard. Sleep got a bit easier the second and third nights as my body adjusted to the cramped conditions.

Then, the morning after my third night, I sensed something had changed with my captors. They were visibly happy, excitable even. The main guy with dark hair and the hippy woman kept coming and going, and they were chatting away like something was about to happen, an urgency to their words.

After an hour or so, the big guy with the comb-over came in and sat next to me.

'Good morning, lad. What a beautiful day it is outside.' He gave me a few jabs with his fork, then dropped it by his feet, bending his head close to mine. 'Don't you just feel happy when the sun comes out?' I shrugged. 'Well, of course,' he leered, 'you can't see it. But you can trust me, the sun is out and it's shining. It's going to be a good day.' Chuckling, he sat back in his chair.

'Keith,' the main guy said from across the room, and the big man glanced up. 'Stop taunting the lad and take him for a piss.'

We went out into the corridor and a warm breeze came at me from the open front door. Two blokes were entering the flat – one of them the grey-skinned man from when I first arrived – carrying a couple of boxes.

'Get a move on,' the guy with the comb-over told me.

I sat on the toilet wondering what they were all getting excited about. Wondering if I could run past this fat bastard and out the front door. Knowing there was no way I could.

Back in the living room, he shut me into my cage then joined the other men at the table. After a few minutes, the hippy woman stuck her head through the doorway.

'Roger's outside,' she said.

All the men promptly left the room, shutting the door behind them.

I could hear their voices move out of the flat. It went quiet for a minute, then the same voices continued, more loudly, more excitedly, from downstairs. It sounded like they were all gathered on the road by the block, a few storeys down from the living room window.

Then I saw a mistake they'd made: the fork, the thing that had been stinging my arse for the last few days, was between the cage and the armchair, where the big guy had left it when he started taunting me. Taking me to the toilet, he'd obviously forgotten to pick it up. I stretched my fingers as far as I could through the cage bars and managed to get it between my finger and thumb, then I slipped it gently towards me and through the bars at the bottom of the cage.

Straight away, I set to on the padlock. I shoved one of the prongs into the keyhole and moved it up and down, in every direction, as hard as I could, desperately hoping that I'd be able to bust it off.

Instead, incredibly, I managed somehow to pick the lock and it popped open with a click. I grabbed my clothes from beside the sofa where they'd chucked them, threw my jeans and t-shirt on as fast as I could, then headed to the door on the other side of the room. As I'd guessed, it led into the kitchen and I raced over to the sink and up onto the worktop. Just like the kitchen in my flat, it faced the field – the other side of the block from the road and where they all were. I didn't stop to think, just knew instinctively to climb out the window, swing over the railings and shimmy down to the next level of flats, just like I did at home when I was avoiding Gary Michaels.

Once I got to the bottom of the flat block, I edged round the side of the building and saw them – the woman, the main guy, the big one who stupidly left the fork – all stood next to a white Escort van, talking with another man who had a dark beard. I ran back down the side and over to my block, out the back of that and onto the main road. It was Monday morning and, like the guy had said, a nice day. I took a punt that Darren and Pete would be over at the shopping precinct where we sometimes hung out. And, sure enough, they were: sitting on the roof, smoking in the sun.

'Alright, mate?' Darren said, as I climbed up to them.

'Alright, lads.'

I sat down and took a cigarette from Pete.

*

Later that night, when I briefly saw her, Shirley didn't ask where I'd been the last three nights. And it didn't occur to me to tell her what had happened. In fact, I didn't bother telling anyone. I understand now that any normal kid would have needed to tell someone, but that wasn't how I thought. I was free, why would I talk about something that was over and done with?

I did wonder – and still do – what the hell those men and that woman would have done to me if I hadn't been able to reach that fork. I guess they were molesters, but they could have been selling kids as slaves, maybe. The Kenny lad was obviously their 'property', doing just as he was told. In the same way that I'd never seen him around before, I never saw him on the estate again.

6

THE VAN

Dr Greenberg: *When something is bothering you, do you like to talk to others about it?*

The next morning I came out of my flat ready to go to school. I was wearing the same clothes I'd had on the day before, nothing unusual there, and I was probably thinking about whether I needed breakfast from Phillip Dean's or not. I wasn't preoccupied by the events from the night before. I wasn't scared or worried or traumatised. Like always, it was something that had happened, no point lingering on it.

I trundled down the concrete stairs of our flat block and across the field on to Crossfield Road. Parked straight across from me was a white Escort van that looked just like the one I'd seen the night before outside the other tower block. Two men stood next to it, both staring at me, though I didn't recognise either of them.

Instantly, not wanting to take any chances, I

turned round and started walking back towards my block, pretending to search in my bag like I'd forgotten something I needed for school. Every couple of steps, I checked over my shoulder to make sure the men weren't following me, but they'd stayed where they were, still just watching.

They must have had it all worked out beforehand. When I got close to the block and I turned my head back again, someone else grabbed me from the front. It was the main guy from the flat, with the thick black hair.

I tried to yell out, but he clamped his hand over my mouth and, with his other hand wrapped firmly across my chest, hefted me over to the van, the doors now open and the two men standing on either side. He threw me in and one of them slammed the doors shut fast.

Within seconds I heard the front doors of the van both snap shut and the engine start. I'd been on my knees and fell backwards as we moved, rocking around in the dark on my back like a beetle.

I tried to concentrate as the van shook me around. But the dark was disorientating and I couldn't tell if we were turning left or right. For a while we drove straight and steady. I kicked the sides to try and make people walking along the street hear, but for all I knew we were driving along the motorway. I slumped back and leant against the side, my whole body vibrating with the engine and every bump in the road.

After a few more minutes the van came to a stop, but the engine kept on running and no one got out. While I could get my footing, I stood up and felt around the back doors. My hand found a lever. You can't imagine the relief that filled me when I pulled it and the doors swung open. Just as the van started to roll forward, I jumped out onto the road. Without stopping to check the cars around me, I ran to my left and into a shop that had its door open. My heart banging blood around my ears, I peered through the shop window and watched the van disappear away from the traffic lights where we'd been stopped, its door swinging on its hinges as they bumped along the road. I jogged out of the shop and down an alley by the side of it, making my way along the back roads that ran parallel to Liverpool Road. I knew the area pretty well and wasn't too far from school – just a bit past it, in fact – so I got on my way to class, walking back the way I'd just been driven. The kidnappers, in my eight-year-old mind, had simply saved me a bit of the walk and, like the night before, I told no one what had happened. I didn't think about telling a teacher, and I certainly wasn't going to tell the lads. What would I say: a load of men kidnapped me because they were angry that I'd gotten away from them – a few days ago they made me strip off and stuck me in a dog cage? Not bloody likely. I did walk a different, much longer route to school for a while, though.

*

The only other time I saw – or, at least, thought I saw – any of those men again in the Manchester area was the day Adam died, several months later.

I never got ill as a child. I vaguely remember having chickenpox at one point, but nothing done about it and it cleared itself up once I stopped scratching at the spots. Other than that, I was surprisingly healthy for someone who went hungry most nights. But I was lucky. Death seemed quite prevalent amongst us kids in Irlam.

Phillip Dean's skin disease got a lot worse when he was nine, and he disappeared one day from school, never to return. And Marie Piechota had some strange hole in her heart that killed her not long after Phillip died. These child deaths must have been devastating to their family and friends, but even at that young age I took them for what they were: part of life.

Adam Kirby's death wasn't as simple to deal with as a disease or a deformity, though. When he died, I experienced a strange sensation that reawakened itself in me fairly recently. Again, there's nothing I can do about it now, so I'm not going to lose sleep, but there's a slight gnawing feeling there that I had when he died. Guilt.

I met Adam on the corner of my flat block one cold Tuesday. He was waiting for me, like he did sometimes, so we could get the bus together, though we went to different schools and he got off way before I did. Although he was a year and a half younger than me, I didn't mind doing this – he was always a bit easier to get on with than his brothers, who were closer to my age, because he didn't expect as much from me. He was happy to just mess about and be relaxed, not constantly needing to prove his toughness.

'Alright?' he said.

I walked up next to him and he punched me on the arm like we were drinking mates down the pub. It was the way we all greeted each other, being mature, not like the other kids around us who'd call each other babyish nicknames.

'Not bad,' I said, and punched him back, harder.

We started walking down to the main road. As we strolled, Adam began digging in his school bag. It was a one-shoulder thing and he'd swung it round to his front so he could see better. He fell a pace or two behind me.

'I haven't done my homework for Mr. Hamlin,' he said. 'And he's a right bastard.'

'Yeah?' I muttered, pretending to be listening.

'Think I best do it on the bus.'

'Right.'

He pulled a brown exercise book from his bag. 'There's ten spellings, and they're really hard.'

I glanced over my shoulder and saw him open the book up.

'Put that away, will you?'

He was going to get beaten up for studying on the bus. And I'd probably get it as well just for being with him.

We got almost to the junction opposite the flat and I glanced left down the road.

'Shit, the bus is coming, come on,' I shouted, quickening my steps.

I looked right and stopped dead in my tracks on the edge of the kerb. A small white van was speeding down the road towards us, going way too fast. In that split second, as it veered closer to us, I didn't have time to move back from the road, to get out of the way, and the very tip of the van's wing-mirror scraped across my stomach. Then there was the biggest bang I've ever heard in my life.

I turned and watched Adam fly up into the air. His exercise book shot out of his hands. His bag came free from his shoulders. He somersaulted across the roof of the van with two loud thuds. The bag kept on going, up and up with the velocity. And Adam landed behind the vehicle as it sped away, twenty-odd feet from where I stood – I could see now, it was a white Escort.

Everything was silent around me.

This was my fault.

The van must have been meant for me. The way it sped up. The way it came right at us, too close to the kerb.

And I'd told him to hurry up when he was distracted by his book. It must have been the molesters, back to get me.

Not Adam.

Without looking again at the mess of his body on the tarmac, I walked across the road to where the bus had stopped, a little further on from where we were.

Behind me, some woman screamed and I heard shouts for help and running footsteps as people obviously rushed over from the estate to Adam's body.

As I got on the bus, I prayed for it to just leave, for no one to have noticed. And, amazingly, the bus began to pull out of the stop. The driver must have been distracted by pulling over and not witnessed what had happened. Or maybe he didn't want the hassle of getting involved himself, and so was choosing to ignore it. I found a boy I knew from my class and sat next to him. He immediately started telling me about football, how Man-U were doing, and City. I didn't say anything; I definitely didn't tell him what I'd just seen. I just sat there. Knowing it should have been me.

*

That afternoon, after school, I went straight home instead of hanging out with my mates as usual. I was tired and needed some sleep. As I opened the flat door, Shirley was just on her way out.

'I saw you out the window this morning, with that Kirby kid,' she said.

'Yeah?' I was sure I was about to get a hiding for just leaving him there, or for not being the one the van hit in the first place.

'Why didn't you take the day off school?' she asked.

A blank expression obviously covered my face because she rolled her eyes.

'Stupid kid. That's the kind of thing you get a day off school for, you know.'

The thought had never occurred to me. Why would *I* get a day off school because *Adam* had been hit by a speeding van?

Shirley shrugged. I knew that meant the conversation was over and I realised that, amazingly, I wasn't going to get the belt. She slung on her leather jacket and left the flat.

For the next couple of weeks, Adam's bag hung, like a deathly reminder, from the lamppost it had wrapped itself around as it fell back down to earth.

7

TAKING AN INTEREST

Dr Greenberg: Do you prefer hobbies that are solitary pursuits?

For a child with anhedonia, it is very difficult to decipher the good in life, because I felt no interest in anything, no enjoyment. This naturally gave more focus to the bad things: problems had to be solved, issues had to be overcome. And, because I didn't know I had anhedonia, there was the confusion over why my mates enjoyed everything, when I didn't. Why they got the feeling of pleasure from cigarettes, when I got the feeling of smoke going in and out. Why they got excited when playing football, when I just got tired. Why finding a pound on the floor made them sing and dance, when I would just give it away.

I had the general idea that someone, somewhere (like a god) had it in for me, and that's why I didn't experience things the way others did, and why I had so much bad luck. But I can see it wasn't all hard going. There were some times of relief in my childhood – not happiness, as such, but breaks from the constant trials of problem solving.

CINEMA TRIPS

Our cinema trips would be organised during school, whispering about what we'd see whilst the teacher scraped chalk across the blackboard in front of us. We would go most Saturdays to the old picture house in Monton, Eccles. We'd catch the bus from the stop just past where Adam got run over, using money I'd pinched from Shirley's tin, or that we'd taken from the gas meters. The ride took about twenty minutes and we'd sit at the back, smoking and throwing things, at each other and out the windows.

The driver would stop right outside the shopping arcade at the front of the cinema. To us, the place was huge. A massive brick building from the 1920s, with grand steps leading up to three sets of double doors. We'd try to sneak one of us in under another's jacket – pretending we were just really fat, not two kids together – or with one of us crawling amongst the others' feet, though we always got caught. Then we'd buy a few sweets to share and get into the screen. There'd be two films showing – the Saturday Matinees, we called them – and we'd stay for both. I remember seeing an early Spiderman movie, and *The Cat from Outer Space*. That was one of the better ones, because it had a cat in it (I've always had an understanding of cats: their motives are simple and clear to read, and they have no expectations). We'd go at least one Saturday a month between the ages of six and ten, and must have seen tons of films. Not that we actually watched much of the films themselves. We'd be too busy throwing sweets at each other, and at the other kids in the audience, and generally mucking around.

Though I don't remember actually *enjoying* myself, I can see that those Saturday Matinees were something good that happened to me. At least, they kept me out of other trouble.

THE CIRCUS

Then there was the time the circus came to town. Something I had never experienced before. Something different. Something potentially interesting.

Everyone in school was excited, it was all the lads could talk about the entire week leading up to the event. After school one night, we all watched the big top being put up in the field, hordes of men pulling on ropes to get the massive red tent standing tall and proud. We could see the cages that held all the animals out the back, though couldn't see inside, and every so often got a glimpse of a woman in a feathered costume, or a clown in full make-up. The lads were almost wetting themselves with anticipation. I looked on passively, but with a curiosity.

The weekend edged closer and I plucked up the courage to ask Mum for the entrance fee on the Friday. She told me no, under no circumstances was I getting my hands on her cash to waste at something like that. She hid her money tin and I had to accept that I wasn't going to go.

I didn't accept it.

Saturday night came around. I knew the field was muddy, from where all the circus performers had been traipsing through all week long, and so I searched the flat for something to wear on my feet other than my torn trainers. When I came across Cath's pink wellies, I thought they'd do: it was dark out and no one would see. I slipped them on and made my way over to the big top.

By the time I got there, cheering and brass-band music was coming from the circus tent, loud as anything, the show well underway. I knew every one of my mates was in there, and all their parents too. It felt like Shirley, Cath and me were the only ones in the town not present. I ran up to the tent and carefully lifted the tarpaulin, sneaking quietly underneath, checking around me the whole time that no one was looking. Sure enough, I got in unnoticed.

The tent had a huge, circular clearing at the front, where a man dressed all in black was standing, a lion in front of him, posing on a box. Eight semi-circular rows of wooden chairs filled the rest of the tent, people jammed in next to each other. But where I'd entered, hardly anyone was sitting. I quickly jumped on a chair at the front and started clapping along with the audience as the lion tamer led the lion around the ring. As he got close to me he stopped and began shouting to us that he was going to do the impossible in a few minutes and something or other.

But I wasn't listening. The lion was moving restlessly on the spot and suddenly lifted his tail, his arse directed at the chair next to me. Then he sprayed. The force at which his urine came out, backwards, was immense and not only did the chair take a covering, but so did I.

The whole audience began to laugh, as the lion and his tamer walked on.

Before I could do anything, or even think about doing anything, an Indian fire breather had come out of an opening in the tent and paraded himself around the audience calling for an assistant. He saw me sat alone and pulled me up next to him, standing me in the centre of the brightly lit ring for all to see. The lion's spray was dripping from my hair, my clothes were soaked down one side and I had the pink wellies still on my feet.

'Hold this,' the fire breather said in a Liverpudlian accent, turning and handing me a burning torch.

He blew two rounds of fire before telling me how bad I stank and that I should get the fuck away from him. I went home and washed myself down in the sink, scrubbing at my lion-stained clothes, realising the circus wasn't that interesting, after all.

THE CHOPPER

The Christmas Eve after Adam got run over, not long before I turned nine, we went to Nan and Grandad's house. They'd come to ours for one or two Christmases before, but we'd never been to theirs on Christmas. This meant I was going to have to stay indoors and do what they wanted to do for at least two days, the whole time Shirley putting on her nice daughter show for their benefit.

As soon as I walked through the flat door on Christmas Eve lunchtime, as Shirley had instructed that morning, she pulled Cath and me into the kitchen and drummed it into us that we had to be on best behaviour, or else. After the usual haircut, followed by the quick wash in the kitchen sink, Shirley gave us some clothes to wear. I couldn't believe it when she handed me a pair of dark blue jeans, all crisp and new, and a navy blue, woolly jumper. She made me put a white shirt underneath with a red tie, but I didn't care. For once, I wasn't dressed like an idiot going to see Nan and Grandad. And I reckoned I could keep these jeans after to replace my current ones that were gaping at the crotch.

Shirley did my tie up neatly for me, without snapping at my failed attempt. She didn't even tell me off when I pulled the knot to loosen it a bit, just calmly said:

'Leave it be, it's festive.'

Then the three of us filed out of the flat, along the landing and down the stairwell. We stood in the frosty air, watching our breath clouding in front of us, all stamping our feet and hugging our hands under our armpits to get warm, none of us wearing a winter coat. All of the flats around us were lit up in the dim afternoon light and I wanted to be inside, out of the cold and doing something useful.

After fifteen minutes of shivering, an immaculate black Ford Zephyr pulled up.

'You bloody took your time,' Mum said to the

driver, as she opened the passenger door.

She swung herself into the front, pulling at her short skirt to stop herself from flashing the whole estate.

'Get in, then,' she said, before closing the door behind her.

Cath opened the back up and slid across the red leather seat. I followed her, pulling the heavy door carefully shut behind me. It smelt of stale fags and aftershave inside, an overpowering mix.

In the driver's seat was a big man I'd never seen before who looked about ten years older than Mum. He turned in his seat, glaring from Cath to me, his eyes deeply sunk into his head. His brown hair was all slicked back with gel, showing just how badly he was receding, and he had a weird smile on his face. I glanced down to see Mum's hand on his upper thigh, her fingers melding with his dark black jeans. The man turned back to the steering wheel and put the car in gear, flicked on the radio and set off.

Christmas songs and radio talk filled the car for the journey, as we all sat in silence. Mum's hand never moved from the man's leg.

Cath gazed out of her window, so I did the same, watching the fields blur past us, and the houses, and then more fields, the light fading quickly until we were driving in darkness, only the lights of houses dotted about. The further we went, the more I could smell petrol fumes and by the time we arrived at Nan and Grandad's little bungalow I was feeling sick.

Just as when Nan and Grandad came to ours, Mum put on her vague smile as soon as they opened the door. She kissed her mother and hugged her father then stepped back.

'This is Frank,' she said to Nan. 'He's a friend of mine who kindly drove us over.'

Frank. I didn't think friends drove with a friend's hand on their leg, but okay.

Grandad showed us all in. Their place was always so clean and tidy and smelled of flowers. After we'd sat for a bit of time in the kitchen, drinking tea and eating sandwiches, the adults talking about I don't know what, and asking me and Cath the odd question about school, Nan said it was time for us to go to bed. Mum gave a glare that said 'don't argue' and my sister and I stood up, following Nan out of the room. She packed both Cath and me off with a hot water bottle and a pair of new pyjamas each, and put me in a sleeping bag at the end of Cath's bed, telling us we had to go to sleep right away, or else Father Christmas wouldn't come. We didn't tell her that we'd never believed.

The next morning, Cath and I woke up to Nan opening the door.

'Merry Christmas!' She stepped over me and pulled open the curtains. 'Rise and shine, there's porridge waiting for you in the kitchen.'

We trundled along the hall after Nan, still in our pyjamas, and sat next to each other at the kitchen table, watching Nan stirring the pot on her stove. Shirley and Frank followed us in about ten minutes later, Mum in striped cotton pyjamas with her short hair stuck on end, and Frank dressed in the clothes he'd come in: a black t-shirt that clung to his belly and black jeans with big heavy boots. They sat opposite me and Cath and we all ate the porridge Nan gave us.

As soon as the dishes were cleared away, Grandad pushed back his chair and stood up, rubbing his hands together.

'Right, who's joining me in the living room?' he asked, his Yorkshire accent strong and full of happiness.

I reluctantly followed Grandad, Shirley and Cath out of the kitchen. Strangely, I liked our Christmases at home on our own, when I could go out and do as I wanted. I hated having to feign enjoyment and get excited over presents that I didn't care about anyway. That kind of emotional reaction just wasn't in me and I didn't like hurting people's feelings with my lack of emotion – as I had when Nan and Grandad had given me presents before: 'Don't you like it?' Nan had asked when I opened the Evel Knievel stunt bike toy one year; I tried so hard to tell her it was nice, yet she still looked disappointed.

There was no Christmas tree in the living room, but Nan had pinned bits of tinsel over the mantelpiece and put a pile of presents in front of her ornament cabinet, all neatly wrapped in red paper dotted with small pictures of lanterns and wreaths. Up against one of the velvety pink armchairs, was a bright red Chopper bike, Grandad standing proudly to one side of it.

'Merry Christmas, Michael,' he said, as I walked in. Seeing my blank expression, he went on: 'This is for you! What do you think?'

I could see Grandad was so happy to be giving me

a bike and I knew this was an expensive present – one I should be ecstatic to be getting – so I tried my hardest to look convincingly happy too. I fixed a smile on my face, showing my teeth to make it seem even better. 'Wow, that's great. Thank you, Grandad.'

'It's from Father Christmas, you know,' Nan said behind me.

'Wow, that's great,' I said again, lost for anything else to say. Then I had a brainwave: 'I need to go and give it a try, can I?'

Thankfully, Grandad immediately started wheeling the bike through the living room and out into the hallway, saying, 'Of course you can. But you best get dressed first or your Nan'll have a fit.'

I ran through to our bedroom at the back of the bungalow and threw on my new jeans, shirt and jumper, being as quick as I could – not out of excitement, but in case they changed their minds about me going out.

They were all waiting in the hallway for me, and everyone shuffled out the front door behind me, Grandad and the bike. Nan told me to tuck my jeans into my socks so I didn't bring myself off. I cycled up and down the street a few times, with Nan and Grandad cheering each time I passed, Shirley whispering in Frank's ear, and Cath shivering in her pyjamas. On my fourth run past the house, I stopped and asked if I could stay out. Shirley's face contorted at my insolence, but Grandad agreed before she could say anything.

'Just keep checking back here to see if dinner's ready,' Nan called after me as I rode off again.

They all went back inside and left me to explore.

This wasn't a bad present: it was practical and was going to get me around the place quicker, to school or town or to see the lads. I cycled past the little school next door, where Grandad was still the caretaker, and on past the houses and through the village to the park. I pedalled around for a good hour or two, just killing time, every ten minutes or so going back to the bungalow to see if anyone was waiting outside to call me in. Eventually, I came round the bottom of the street and saw Cath with her arms folded, waiting outside, shivering in her pink dress and thin cardigan.

'You've got to come in,' she shouted. 'Dinner's nearly ready.'

Nan had put on a massive spread and we all sat around the table in the dining room with plates full of turkey and potatoes and sprouts and gravy and cranberry sauce. For afters, there was Christmas pudding and cream that tasted of alcohol. Just like the night before, the adults all chatted and Cath and I sat there being as good as gold in silence.

Once all the plates and leftover food was cleared away we went back through to the living room 'to digest', as Grandad put it. Everyone else had opened their presents while I was out and they were spread across the living room, along with the discarded wrapping paper. Cath got a special doll, even though she was getting a bit old for dolls now, and a selection box. Mum got some soaps, and she gave Nan a nice handkerchief and Grandad a scarf.

Nan and Grandad's living room was very different from ours. They had pink flowery wallpaper that matched the sofa and armchairs, and even had rugs over the thick carpet. It was a comfortable room to be in, especially with the gas fire going and bellies full of Christmas dinner, so I didn't mind that I had to stay in for the rest of the afternoon. I caught Shirley's eye as I went to sit on one of the armchairs. She glared at me and I quickly changed my mind, plonking myself on the floor in front of the TV instead. Grandad put the Christmas matinee on for Cath and me to watch. It was *Custer of the West*, one I hadn't seen, but the grown-ups talked all the way through so I couldn't even hear what Robert Shaw was saying. After the film, Frank said it was starting to get dark, which meant we should be heading back to Manchester.

Before the bike was bundled into the boot of the Zephyr, some old rope tying it down ready for our long drive home, I had to pose for the obligatory boy-on-his-new-bike photo outside Nan and Grandad's bungalow.

'Smile,' Grandad said, stood in the street and clutching a leather-clad camera to his face.

I steadied myself with one foot on the ground, then put my hands on the handlebars and tried my hardest to look happy once again.

A HOBBY

Daniel Wright and I occasionally went to the straw fields across the main road from the estate, to dig up the earth, trying to find old coins and bottles with marbles in the neck of them buried in the ground. It was a challenge between us to see who could find the oldest ones. Daniel loved it: he would get really excited when we found a coin that was older than 1900. He spent hours at his kitchen table cleaning the mud and grime off them till they shone. I collected them because he did; this was his hobby, not mine. I kept my bottles in a row on the set of drawers in my room, mud still clinging to the edges, and the coins in a grey fabric bag next to the bottles, never getting them out again.

When Daniel wasn't about, and there was no one else to hang around with, I'd sometimes go to the fields on my own and that's where I discovered *my* hobby. I'd pinch matches from the drawer in our kitchen and then, in the field, I'd pick a strand of straw and set it alight, watching it burn. It was like I was giving life by igniting it and creating this flame. There was something magical about the flickering light, the oranges and yellows that came from this little piece of burning straw. And I loved the warmth it gave off. But as the flame would start to burn out, I felt like something was dying. I suddenly needed to keep it alive and so I'd add another strand of straw, and then another and another, just to keep my little flame alive.

Inevitably, it wasn't long before I set the farmer's field alight.

I tried to stamp it out at first. But my shoes were always flapping with holes and had no capability of putting out a fire without burning off my foot. So I watched as the flames took hold of the straw stalks growing through the earth, the fire spreading a few inches left and right, then a few feet. Then I knew I was in trouble and I jumped on my red Chopper bike and pedalled off down the lanes, through the houses, until the burning field was forgotten.

I don't know how many times this happened in my childhood. It certainly wasn't once. The flames had some kind of power over me, capturing my attention in a way nothing else ever did.

8

IN THE CELLS

Dr Greenberg: Are you content to sit alone, just thinking and daydreaming?

It probably won't come as a surprise that I spent a night in a prison cell before I even turned nine. But it wasn't because of the farmer's field burning to the ground. And it wasn't because I'd been stealing pop from the shop in town. Or because I'd smashed someone's window, or played chicken in front of a police car. It was Shirley.

I got home one evening from hanging around with my mates after school and she was waiting for me in the kitchen. She was never usually in during the evenings and so as soon as I saw her I knew trouble was coming. I stood in front of her, my head low, waiting for whatever it was that was coming.

'You've been pinching again, haven't you?' she said.

It was true, I had been taking money from her tin, even though she'd put on a padlock to keep me out. The one thing I learnt that day I got kidnapped by the molesters and thrown into that cage was how to unpick a lock; it really wasn't that difficult. Shirley had a two-pronged fork just like theirs – I have no idea why, because she never did any cooking, but she had one anyway. When she was out, I'd carefully prod that fork into the padlock on her money tin and wiggle it about – just like I had when I was in the cage – until the lock popped open. I'd take a tenner then slip the padlock back on like I'd never been there, ready to buy myself and my mates some cigarettes, or some food down the Rasta café.

Shirley was tight, so of course she spotted the money had gone.

'Been pinching, haven't you?' she repeated.

I shrugged, waiting for the beating to come. The sooner it came, the sooner it would be over.

'I've fucking had enough of it.' She was shouting now. 'You're a dirty little thief. And you know what happens to thieves?'

She suddenly stood up and I got ready for the first blow as she reached out to me. But instead of knocking me sideways, she grabbed hold of my t-shirt at the shoulder and started walking out the door, pulling me behind her. Rather than going to the bedroom for a thrashing like normal, she dragged me to the front door and shoved me out.

'Where we going?' I asked, as she led me along our landing.

'I'm taking you for the police to deal with.'

The whole way to the police station her fingers pinched into my arm as we strode along. When we arrived at the small building, not much more than a hut, Shirley pushed me down onto a chair in the waiting area.

'Excuse me,' she said, all polite, to the balding police officer at the desk. She tucked her hair behind her ear as she continued in a small voice: 'I need you to teach my son a lesson – he's been stealing from me.'

The policeman raised his eyebrows, looked me up and down in my ripped and dirty clothes and tutted loudly.

'Has he? We can't have that, can we?' He strolled out from behind the desk and stood over me, legs apart, hands on his hips and his stomach bursting at the buttons of his dark blue jacket. He stank of B.O. 'So you've been stealing from your own mother. That doesn't sound very nice now, does it?'

'Not just once either,' Shirley piped up from behind him, and he twisted to see her. 'He does it all the time. He's really naughty and there's nothing I can do to stop him. I'm on my own, you see.'

The officer gave a sigh of sympathy for this poor single mother, then turned from her to me. 'In this life, son, theft is rewarded with jail time. It's best you learn this early. A common thief like you can sample a life of crime with the same treatment all those other thieves get: a night in the cells. What do you say to that?'

As a kid, I was always polite to people in authority (teachers, friends' parents, and so on), but I didn't see how this fat, balding, sweaty, arrogant man deserved my respect just because he was in a uniform.

'Go on then,' I said.

The officer stared at me. 'Go on then?' He laughed. 'You really are something, aren't you? You won't be so cocky after a night with us.' He turned back to Shirley, who was now primping the back of her hair with her fingers. 'That okay with you, Miss?'

'You'll be doing me a favour,' Shirley said. 'Take him.' She pushed away from the desk and sauntered out of the station.

The officer watched her leave, before leaning down to me, his nose half an inch from mine, the smell of his sweat increasing. 'Children,' he started, his voice increasing with every syllable, 'should not steal from their own mothers. Get up!'

I stood from my seat. I'd never been in a police station before and never even spoken to a police officer. This man was big and tall. If Mum could knock me off my feet, I couldn't imagine how bad a beating from him was going to be.

'Get through there,' he shouted, pointing to a corridor behind his desk.

I did as I was told, scared of what I was about to get, wondering if I should have been quite as cheeky as I was.

A barred cell was at the back of the station, the desk still in sight of it. The officer unlocked the door and pushed me roughly inside, then locked it back up again. I stood at the bars, the officer no more than a foot away from me, but on the outside: he couldn't hurt me like this.

'You're a disgusting waste of space. Your mother was right to bring you here, a night in the cells will break you right down. You'll think twice next time before you go nicking from her purse.'

'It wasn't her purse,' I said.

'Are you questioning me? Don't you dare say another word, or I'll make this far worse for you. You sit there–' he pointed to a metal bed that was held to the back wall with big brackets '–and you think about what you've done. You think on it till the morning.'

And so I sat there, on the thin blue mattress, my back against the wall, my legs stuck out in front of me. I was used to being on my own; the officer wasn't going to hurt me: this wasn't so bad. All I had to do was wait it out, so I focussed on the task and forget about everything else. Every so often, different policemen would appear and talk to the one on the desk. They'd glare over at me, sneer, shout out a bit of weak abuse, then get on with whatever they were doing. All the while, I just sat and waited, as I'd been told (though I didn't think about what I'd done). In a way, the police were only doing their job – like Mr Granger's punishments – and I understood that. In fact, they were doing my mum a favour. Which, I realised, was kind of nice.

When the morning arrived, Shirley drifted back in at about ten o'clock. There were two different men on the front desk now and I watched both of them nudge each other under the counter.

'I'm here for my son,' Shirley said, craning her neck to see me in the back. 'Has he been much bother?'

'No, he's just sat there the whole time. Not said a word. Didn't even sleep, apparently.'

'Probably too scared,' the other officer said, and they all chuckled.

The shorter of the two got up from his seat and came and let me out, then guided me to the front of the station.

'What have you got to say to your mother?' the officer behind me said.

I glanced at Shirley, unsure of what I was supposed to say. She looked as though she'd been up all night, still in a short skirt and her make-up a bit smudged around her eyes.

'I don't have time for all that,' Shirley said. 'I'm sure he's learnt his lesson. Come on.'

She steered me out of the station and I realised that she'd probably had something on last night, something she wanted me out of the way for: the police were just glorified babysitters to her.

We walked back to the flat in silence.

'Let yourself in,' she said, as we approached the block. 'I've got somewhere to be. And don't even think about going in that tin.'

I went straight in and took out two notes, then went to call for Daniel. Maybe she had meant to scare me. But, if that was the worst she could do, it wasn't so bad.

9

THIS IS LIFE

Dr Greenberg: Say you move to a new city, would you have a strong need to make new friends?

Getting through the days without emotion made my life easier as a child. It meant that I really didn't care that my mother had little interest in me. I didn't mind that my clothes were that much worse than my friends', they did me well enough. I didn't mind that I didn't have the few toys or games that my friends had, because they don't serve a practical purpose anyway. The hunger wasn't an issue, because I had no interest in food, and I usually found something to eat if I was desperate, because I had my network to turn to. They were all I needed to stay alive, and to stop me from going mad with boredom. And that was fine by me.

But, in the space of one day, my network disappeared.

I was eleven and junior school was one week from finishing for the summer; in September I would be starting at Irlam and Cadishead High. That Friday afternoon, I walked home from school and found Shirley waiting with her friend Frank next to a big white van, just outside our block. Cath was already sitting in the cab, still wearing her school uniform, her face mardy as anything.

'What's going on?' I asked, as I got close.

'Finally, you're here.' Shirley pushed herself off the side of the van where she'd been leaning and slipped onto the seat next to my sister.

'Get in the back,' Frank said to me.

'Why?'

'Just do it.' He grabbed hold of my shoulder and pushed me round to the back of the van, so roughly I was almost tripping over my feet.

Inside was all our stuff. Everything Shirley, Cath and I owned. Our sofa, the TV, the kitchen table and chairs, our beds, chest of drawers, and a load of black bags. I could see one of Mum's flowery dresses sticking out the top of one bag, a cream woolly jumper coming out of another. Somewhere in there must have been my clothes too.

I glanced up at our flat – the front door shut firm. Margaret from the flat below ours was standing on her landing, watching us. She wiped at her cheeks as I stared at her, and I realised she was crying, then she started waving. I raised my hand to wave back, but Frank shoved my shoulder and I stumbled into the van's bumper. With another quick push, he forced me to clamber in amongst our stuff. The van shutter slammed down behind me, and seconds later the vehicle juddered into motion.

I sat down quickly as we started to move, wedging myself between the small set of drawers from my bedroom and the green armchair from the lounge. Above my head the thick, blue plastic roof of the van trapped in the summer heat. It was unbearable from the first minute: suffocating and humid. Every corner he took, Frank seemed to swing the van as hard as he could, rocking our stuff up and down and side to side, and me with it all. Sickness rose up in me, from the pit of my stomach, collecting at the bottom of my throat, churning every time I moved backwards and forwards. The drive seemed to go on forever, though it could only have been around forty minutes, and I lost all sense of direction, no idea of where we were headed. When the van finally stopped, Frank came round and let the shutter up.

'Out,' he commanded.

And I followed, thankful to leave the sticky, sweaty heat and have a blast of fresh air to settle the sickness in my guts.

Two rows of terraced, brand new houses stood in front of me, a path of grass separating them down the middle. All of the walls were clad with wood, the windows were thick white plastic and each house had a corrugated roof and corrugated porch at the front. A grassy bank led up to the houses and behind me trees lined the street, with more behind the terraces.

'This is where you live now,' Shirley said, walking round to the back of the van, Cath following her. 'Help us get the stuff in the house, you two.'

I'm sure any normal child would have been excited to see a whole house that they were going to live in, on a nice street, with trees and everything.

But I wasn't an average child and I was in shock.

'What are you doing?' I said, my head full of thoughts about the home we'd just left behind, miles and miles away. 'I'm not moving!'

Shirley, reaching a key out of the back pocket of her jeans, walked over to the last house of the terrace next to the dividing alley – a number twenty-seven hanging from the porch – and unlocked the dark wood front door.

'Hey!' I shouted, running after her, annoyance flickering in my head. 'Take me back, now. You can't do this to me.'

'Yeah, I can,' she said. And that was that. Over.

Done.

My feeling subsided.

We all started taking bags and bits of furniture into the house. I tried claiming the largest of the three bedrooms, but, of course, Shirley was having that. Cath got the other big room at the back of the house, and I got the box room at the front. Big enough for a single bed and my small set of drawers.

From the outside, this must have appeared like any normal family, all working together on moving day. But, unlike normal families, we didn't laugh and joke. We didn't even talk to each other. We just got on with it, efficiently, getting the job done.

As soon as everything was out, Shirley and Frank got in the van and drove off, leaving me and Cath in our new house. Cath was still mardy – the move was obviously a surprise to her too – and she shut herself in her room, leaving me to explore our new estate on my own. I searched around for my Chopper bike, but it wasn't anywhere, Shirley had obviously left it in Eccles along with my bag of old coins and bottles, so I started out on foot. All the houses were just like ours: new council builds in the middle of some old forest they'd chopped down. Small, clean and tidy. It was quieter than Manchester. No sirens going off. No kids in the street.

I spent a few hours getting my bearings: a brook ran out the back of our house, through the woods, behind that was a tall metal fence and a train line. I found the local shops at the end of our lane, the playground, the local pub – Nelson's Quarter Deck. There was nothing to do, no one to see. This was Birchwood, a couple of miles outside the centre of Warrington; my network in Manchester was long gone and I didn't know how I was going to cope without it. I went back to the house. Shirley was sat on the sofa with the cat on her lap. I called her a bitch and went to bed.

*

For the first week after we moved, Shirley made me go to school, to see out the end of summer term. She enrolled me at the Catholic Church of Transfiguration junior school, just two minutes' walk from our new house. I had nothing else to do other than attend. That Monday morning, I walked into the school yard, knowing just how things worked, asking who the toughest kid in school was. A boy about half a foot taller than me sidled straight up to me and glared into my face.

'What of it?' he said.

This kid was too tough for me by far. But a smaller, slightly weedier looking lad stood at his shoulder, backing him up. The number two, second in command.

'Nothing, nothing,' I said. I quickly took aim and punched the side-kick.

The big lad stepped out of the way and started chanting 'fight, fight, fight' in his almost-broken voice, and while everyone gathered round, the side-kick pulled himself together and tried to punch me back. But I was too quick. A knock or two later and I was the winner of our sudden fight. The toughest kid in school came over and gave me a nod of approval, and that was me sorted for the week. No trouble was going to come my way with this lad on my side.

In that week of school, I experienced two firsts: my first communion – a man in a dress handing all us kids bits of sweaty bread and juice, whilst giving the teachers little cups of wine at ten in the morning – and my first open-mouthed kiss. Of course, I'd kissed a couple of girls at Moorfield County Primary, but apparently things were different in Warrington. When I tried putting my lips up to this girl's lips, all the other kids laughed at me. 'He isn't opening his mouth!' they taunted. Ever the one to fit in, I quickly learnt what was expected.

A few days after school broke up for the summer I got my first job: a paper round I saw advertised in the window of the local shop. It started with just the morning dailies, but I wanted other routes, to give me something to do and to get more money. I asked Shirley to order me a new bike from the catalogue, promising to pay the weekly instalments. Amazingly, she agreed and once I'd got my racer – I chose the fastest I could afford so I could get around quick – I took on deliveries for the Midweek Guardian, the Friday paper, and the Evening News.

Around that time, Mum got a dog. It was a black Labrador, just a couple of years old, and someone named him Shep. I didn't mind having him around – it was something new, something different – so I let him come on my paper round, running alongside my bike to keep up. The dog doted on me and would wait, looking out of my bedroom room window, whenever I went out without him. I'd get back and he'd still be there, jumping up as I walked through the door.

That whole summer, the paper round was the only thing I had to do. For the first time ever, I had nowhere to go and no one to see, and I had my own money. I spent hours in my bedroom, staring at the ceiling. Some afternoons I'd go next door to see Dot and Les, our elderly neighbours. Dot would usually be baking something and so I'd get fed with whatever was on the go. She'd get me involved as well, folding flour with milk and eggs to make a cake, or cutting scones out of thick, currant-filled dough. I felt okay going over there: women who took care of me always attracted me, not physically, of course, Dot was well over sixty, but because she made me feel comfortable by giving me food and not asking too many questions. Dot's daughter was like that as well, very welcoming and caring, but not too pushy. For a while, I babysat her toddler when she went out, though the kid was always asleep and all I had to do was watch TV and run to get someone if he woke up.

Sometimes I'd sit and watch telly with Frank and

Shirley in the evenings – horror films, like *Texas Chainsaw Massacre* and *The Hills Have Eyes* (another sign of irresponsible parenting, but luckily, because of how I am, these films never disturbed me even though I was only eleven). Frank, I soon worked out, was now living with us. 'The Lodger', as we called him, wasn't exactly a step-dad or Shirley's boyfriend, he was more of a live-in-lover. He'd give my mum money, and in return he shared her bed and our house. But he was a bastard to live with.

After Shirley dragged us away from Eccles, something in me changed. I couldn't forgive what she'd done: I lost all respect for her, and I stopped being afraid of her beatings. One day she gave me some money to go and get a haircut, before a visit from Nan and Grandad, and instead of taking myself to the barber's, I cycled all the way back to Eccles on my racer. I met up with Darren Black and we bought ourselves some cigarettes with Shirley's money, then went back to his and completely shaved my head with his brother's clippers. This caused Shirley to explode when I got in, but I didn't give a shit.

The chances for us to have arguments over small stuff increased no end. She was at home in the evenings (I now see Frank was paying her upkeep, so she didn't need to 'work' at night), which meant there was plenty of time for us to get into a row. At the time, I really couldn't care less what the repercussions would be and so I said whatever I thought. She'd tell me to get to my room and I'd say, 'No, I don't want to.' She'd tell me to get my bike in and I'd say, 'But I'm going out in a minute.' She'd say, 'You're not going out,' and I'd tell her I was.

It was all very well speaking my mind to her, but then Frank would get involved. He was a lorry driver now, but previously Frank was a cop, a dodgy one at that, and he had a Magnum .357 hanging in a holster on the front room wall, always threatening me with its presence. He had some weird Zulu spears hung up too, though he never got them down. I'm sure he loved the rows. Throwing his weight around. Intimidating me. His favourite move was to wait for me to leave the room and, as I walked past him, he'd fling his arm out and backhand me across the face with no warning. I'd stagger into the wall or doorframe, or whatever was next to me. Once he caught me so hard his hand bust my nose. It wasn't broken, but the side split and sent blood down into my mouth.

As soon as I tasted the irony blood, the fear in me went away. I wasn't scared of him because he'd hit me now, what else could he do?

I turned round to him and said: 'You're a big man aren't you? Makes you hard, doesn't it, hitting an eleven-year-old boy.'

I could see the anger swelling in his piggy eyes, his temples tensing and his mouth contracting in on itself, but he let me leave and didn't follow. Only once did he lay into me with any real aggression.

It was after I'd started at the secondary school. I'd been there just a few months and was still coming home after my evening paper round, nowhere else to go. As I opened the front door and stepped into the hallway, Frank was there, a wooden broom in his hand. He must have been standing at the window for ages, just waiting for me to come home.

'It was you!' he shouted in my face and the broom shaft smashed against my chest.

I dodged round him, but he hit me again, thrashing my back as I moved. He dropped the broom and shoved me into the space under the stairs. My legs went from under me and, as I tried to push myself back up off the floor, he punched me square in the face.

'You thief!' he screamed.

Blood streamed from my nostrils and I fell down onto my back. He kicked me, then stood straight, breathing heavily, his face blotched red.

'I'm going to tell the police on you,' I said, wiping at the pouring blood.

'You can't,' he sneered. 'I've got theirs and your mum's permission, you thieving little shit.'

That's when I saw Shirley, standing in the front room doorway, nodding.

'You fucking steal from me, this is what fucking happens,' Frank said.

'But I haven't stolen anything.' I knew he'd got it wrong, I was too scared to steal anything from him, not that I was going to admit that to him.

'Liar! I know it was you. Nicking from my bottle. I've got proof.'

Frank kept an oversized whisky bottle next to the chest of drawers in their room. He put all his loose change in it at the end of every day. Every couple of weeks he liked to count it out at the kitchen table. I glanced through to the kitchen and there was the empty bottle with stacks of coins neatly arranged beside it. Frank saw me looking.

'It wasn't me,' I said. 'I've admitted when I've stolen stuff from Mum before, haven't I? And I'd admit this now if it was me. But it wasn't.'

'You saying it was Cath then?'

I shook my head; we all knew Cath would never steal from either of them.

'I know it was you,' he said again. 'I took it to my mates down the nick earlier. That's right, you little shit. Told them twenty quid was missing, so Gaz fingerprinted it for me. And guess what, there were prints on it that weren't mine – small prints, like yours. You thieving little bastard.' He kicked me in the side and I doubled up, clutching my ribs, as he stormed into the kitchen, slamming the door and leaving Shirley and me in the hall.

Shirley raised her eyebrows, a blankness in her eyes, no sign of sympathy or caring on her face, then she turned and disappeared into the front room to continue watching her programme.

In the bathroom, I washed the blood from around my mouth, pinched the bridge of my nose, the way I'd seen teachers do with kids at school, and sat on the edge of the bath waiting for the blood to stop coming. *It must have been her*, was all I could think. Shirley's hands were just as small as mine. Smaller maybe. It couldn't have been anyone else.

After that, Frank's behaviour towards me changed. It turned into psychological warfare. Some nights, I'd hear a noise and wake up to find him standing over me, staring, the hall light making him into a looming silhouette. Through my fear, I'd try to sound angry, telling him to get out, that he was a weirdo, a perv, but he wouldn't flinch. He'd just stand there, glaring at me, for the longest time, so that when he finally left I'd be too worked up to get back to sleep. At other times, I'd wake up in the morning to find the word *THIEF* typed on the little TV screen that was connected to my ZX Spectrum (bought with my paper round money). Or in my sock drawer there'd be a torn piece of paper with big black letters spelling out *RUNT*. Other times there'd be a note stuck to the wall just above my pillow: *BASTARD*. Those were the ones that scared me the most. How had he got so close in the night, without me noticing?

*

Being at home was something I started to avoid, at least in the evenings; no one was ever there in the daytime. I joined the local Scout group, paying for it with money from my paper round. It wasn't far from where we lived and I thought it would be a good way to meet kids in the area, to start forming my network again. Not only did I want to get out the house, but I also needed some friends to live off (although she was home more, Shirley still didn't bother about feeding me, or Cath). I never really saw her and Frank eat, though I sometimes found their leftovers. Going to Scouts meant I got a few badges, for 'joining in' and some other activities, and I sewed them onto my uniform. I doubt Shirley even knew I was going; if she did, she never said anything.

But praise from her for my 'achievements' wasn't something I was after. I didn't care how well I did, or how many badges I got. Scouts was a device to make useful friends in the area and that was it.

The Scoutmaster, Cliff, took me under his wing – probably after seeing my general neglected appearance he felt sorry for me. He lived in a basement flat just round the corner from ours, and started offering me lifts to and from the Scout hut. Some days I'd meet him round the back of his flat and we'd get straight into his mustard-colour Morris Marina. Other days, he'd ask me to help carry boxes out to the car and I'd go into his little one-bed flat with him, collect what he told me and carry it out. He obviously didn't need any help – he was a fairly tall guy with a strong build and could have managed them easily on his own – but was probably trying to make me feel useful or something. Either way, he asked, so I helped. I'd take them back in for him at the end of the evening too. If he wasn't busy, he'd make me a cup of tea and ask me if there was anything I was struggling with in Scouts. He taught me how to tie reef knots and a highwayman's hitch, and he chatted away to me about all the things we were going to learn that term. I didn't mind his company, it was something to do other than go home and sit with Shirley and Frank.

After around six months of being in Scouts, Cliff started talking about karate, telling me how useful it was and encouraging me to go along. He helped out at a local group and eventually I agreed to give it a go. It became a regular thing: he'd pick me up on a Saturday afternoon, we'd go to the class, then afterwards he'd take me to the pub next door and buy me a Coke, while he had a beer, the froth always getting caught in his wiry moustache. It seemed like I was his protégé, like he was trying to be a mentor: as with Scouts, any difficulties I was having with karate he tried to talk them through with me. What he didn't realise was that I had literally no interest in either Scouts or karate – I really couldn't care less about getting the badges or the belts, I just took part because that was what I had to do if I wanted to get a new network of friends. Spending a bit of extra time with Cliff in his flat or down the pub was an alright price to pay if it meant I got a free Coke and I was out of the house a bit longer.

I actually felt quite bad for the bloke, because he would try so hard with me and I didn't want his help with anything. Ever since I was a little kid, if I didn't know how to do something I would either teach myself or not bother. Because of Shirley's parenting techniques, I was determinedly self-sufficient, so Cliff's mentoring and kindness was utterly wasted on me.

He never realised, though. Our schedule continued for around two months – Scouts on Wednesday night and karate on Saturdays. Then, after Scouts one evening, he asked me to help take a box of clothes over to his friend's house. We drove round to the other side of town and he parked the car at the bottom of this new block of flats that looked like oversized chalets. He handed me a box with a few scarves and activity shorts inside and I followed him into a grubby-looking stairwell, up three flights of wooden stairs to a flat door, which he unlocked.

'Come on in,' Cliff said, over his shoulder, and I followed him inside.

The hallway smelt damp and, even though the flats weren't that old, the wallpaper was peeling off the walls at its seams. We walked through to the living room, which was equally as dishevelled, and he told me to hang on where I was, in the doorway, while he crossed to a table where two middle-aged guys were sitting. He spoke quietly to them as he lay his keys down on the table. I wondered if these men were really Cliff's friends. He always seemed so lonely; it was weird to think he hung out with mates when Scouts and karate weren't on. And all these men were quite scruffy; not like him with his neat, beige Scoutmaster shirt. A couple of other guys were sitting on a sofa that had foam popping out of its sides. As my gaze rested on the man closest to me, he quickly and very deliberately turned his head away. It was such a strange reaction, like he didn't want me to see his face, and I wondered if I'd seen this man with grey-flecked stubble and a balding head before. I thought maybe I recognised him from Manchester. But the thought was fleeting and Cliff was coming towards me.

'This way,' he said, putting his hand lightly on my back and steering me round into the hallway.

We passed two closed doors and went into a small bedroom that had a stack of boxes in the far corner beside the bed. He told me to add the one I was holding to the pile. I did as I was told, then turned around to leave, bumping straight into Cliff. He'd shut the door.

Cliff put his hands round my arms and gently pulled me close to him. Then, in a quick movement, he pushed me down on the bed.

'What are you doing?' I said, confused about why he'd pushed me over.

He leant above me and lifted me off the bed so I

was up close to him again, pulling me into him, close enough that his moustache brushed against my cheek, and then he slammed me down on the bed once more. Then he did it again. And as he pulled me into his body this third time I felt his erect penis jab into my thigh.

I pushed off his chest and landed back on the bed, quickly getting to my feet before he could grab me again.

'What the fuck are you doing?' I raised my voice, tried to appear as big and angry and aggressive as I could, standing over him on the bed. 'Get the fuck off me!'

Cliff, unused to anger in me, stepped back, his lips parted and his eyes searching my face. He was still hard, his penis pushing at the fabric of his trousers, making the fly bulge.

I took my chance and jumped off the bed, flung the door open and raced down the hallway to the front door, desperate to get out before the men in the living room realised what was happening. Amazingly, no one had locked me in and I shot out of the flat, down the three flights of stairs and out to the corner of the street.

I knew there was no way they'd catch me now I was out of the flat: they were all middle-aged and, other than Cliff, all overweight. Cliff could have taken me down when I started to shout at him – he was far bigger and stronger than me – but he was a placid man and I doubted that he would try to chase me at all.

I was right. Of course, I never went to the Scout meets again, or karate, and he didn't try to contact me. On the rare occasion he would see me on the street or in a shop, he would look the other way, or even turn and walk in the opposite direction, so he obviously didn't feel like trying it again.

Just like the times in Manchester, I didn't tell anyone about Cliff's weird advances. It wasn't a deliberate decision not to, it was because it wasn't a problem any more. It didn't play on my mind or bother me; there was no point dwelling on something that had already happened and couldn't be changed. And anyway, who would I tell? I moved on.

10

REBUILDING THE NETWORK

Dr Greenberg: Do you find you become deeply attached to people you spend a lot of time with?

I know now that an average twelve-year-old boy would probably have had nightmares about his Scoutmaster grooming him for sex. They would be emotionally scarred, traumatised, disturbed, in need of counselling. But, thanks to the anhedonia, this has never been the way my brain works. Incidents happen and I deal with them. Once they are over, they are forgotten. There's no lasting damage. I went straight back to wanting a support network around me – none of the kids at karate or Scouts had been much use for that, too goody-goody – and so, like nothing had happened, I decided to try making ground with some of the lads from school.

Nick Sleden was in my year and he and his family were living in the Padgate area, close to the school and about an hour's walk from where I lived. They'd moved to Warrington around the same time as us, and so didn't know many kids either. Nick's house wasn't the biggest in the world, but it was always full of people coming and going – perfect for me to fit in.

I started hanging around with Craig, Nick's older brother – a skinhead who was all muscle, unlike Nick whose clothes were far more important than anything else. Andrew Buxton and Mark Farina, who both lived behind Nick and Craig, hung out with us as well. Andrew had grown up in Warrington, but Mark had come over from America a few years before, his mum was an alcoholic and let him do anything he wanted. We played a lot of five-aside together, and got into our own fair share of trouble as well. The lads liked me because I was amenable. That automatic 'yes' answer was even more apparent now I was in my teens, so I'd go along with any mad plans they had. It gave me something to do, a purpose, and kept me from being bored. We used to camp on the five-aside field some nights, making sure we woke up around 5am, just after the milkman had done his deliveries: he would leave not just milk but bacon, eggs and even sausages in the meter boxes around the estate, so we'd break in and get ourselves enough to cook up a breakfast on a small fire in the middle of the field. Other times, we'd nick stuff from the local shops to eat and drink. The crimes were never that bad, just kids messing around, but whatever trouble there was the lads could be sure I'd go along with it.

The thing is, whenever I was with these guys I'd generally get fed and handed cigarettes, because I was there and they were eating and smoking, so it was natural that they'd share with me. I'd have a bed to crash in if I didn't want to go home, and I had company at any time of the day I wanted. They were my new network and I was their new 'yes' man; it was an equally beneficial friendship all round.

And that's what I needed, because, by the time I was thirteen, home life was abysmal. I stayed at my mates' houses a lot of the time – at Craig's, Mark's and Andrew's – but there were nights I had to go home to give my mates some rest from me. I'd sneak in our front door and silently creep up the stairs to my bedroom, avoiding going downstairs again unless I really had to. In the morning I'd get up early, have a quick shower and get out before either Frank or Mum saw me. If they did see me, an argument would begin immediately.

Though I don't have the emotional capacity to get angry for a sustained period of time, if Shirley got mad at me I would mimic her behaviour, raising my voice equally as loud as hers and using the same language she used towards me. We'd scream and shout at each other and then Frank would throw his two-pence in; later I'd have to contend with his mind games. I know now that I wasn't an easy child to live with, that my hostile, belligerent attitude wound up and angered Shirley, but back then I just thought they were against me for the sake of it.

Cath wasn't around to witness much of this. She spent most of her time at Jack's house – a lad she met that first summer we were in Warrington and her childhood sweetheart, who she eventually married. I thought Jack was a fairly decent guy and occasionally I'd hang around with them. He liked to have a laugh with me, like dangling me off the motorway overpass by my ankles when I was annoying him, or getting me to try smoking weed, which I really didn't see the point of (it only made me want to sit and do nothing, and that was something I hated to do). Cath usually stayed at Jack's place, but when she did come home she would lock her bedroom door with a big padlock Shirley had given her. I always thought it was to keep me out, to stop me from stealing from her room (not that I would have, but they didn't know that). But, talking with Cath as adults, I've discovered the lock was to keep out Frank, not me. As far as I know, he never raped her, but he did try it on a few times. I guess he wanted Cath as an added extra, on top of Shirley's services. At least Shirley had the decency to stop that from happening.

The way she eventually dealt with me didn't show the same duty of protection. When I was thirteen, I went home one night straight after school and Mum strode out of the house to meet me, before I'd even gone up the front path. Without saying a word, she grabbed hold of my arm and started pulling me back down the lane, her nails digging into my skin through my school jumper. I tried asking her what she was doing, where we were going, but she didn't speak, just kept marching on ahead, her face hard and unflinching.

We came to a halt at the bus stop and I realised we weren't heading to the police station like last time – we could have walked there easily. As the bus pulled up, she sharply told me to get on. I stepped up and she bought us two tickets into town. We sat side by side near the back of the bus, me next to the window, her pinning me in, staring straight ahead.

'Mum,' I said, trying to read the expression on her face. 'Can you just tell me where we're going?'

She looked ahead.

'Has something happened? …Do you think I've done something? Cause I haven't… Just tell me and I promise I'll tell you the truth. I always do, don't I?'

I thought I could see tears beginning to well in her eyes, but she kept on staring forward, her eyes flicking between the cars and lorries and busses on the other side of the road; the traffic lights turning from red to amber to green; pedestrians strolling along the street, some in suits, some in trackies; anything, but me. I didn't like that she wasn't answering my questions, or that she was ignoring me. And I couldn't work out what was going on.

'Mum, where are we going?' I tried one last time, but still nothing.

I gave up and gazed out the window at the shops we moved past. It was rush hour and the journey seemed to take twice as long as it normally would. We got off at the bus station and she immediately clutched hold of my arm again.

'Alright,' I said, trying to shrug her off. 'I'm coming with you, let go.'

But she kept a firm hold. We walked around the perimeter of the newly finished Golden Square shopping centre and on to Sankey Street, the grand Town Hall and all its park land ahead of us. Then we crossed over to Hilden House, home to the housing association and social services lot. I wondered if we were moving to another town again, if she'd got sick of Frank and was leaving him. But then, surely, she would have brought Cath with us.

'This way,' she said, marching me through the

double doors and into the foyer.

Letting go of my arm, Shirley stomped over to the desk and said something to the receptionist that I couldn't hear. The receptionist left her seat and disappeared into the back.

All over the walls were posters for government schemes and benefits and housing and welfare and health. Two wire stands were stacked full of leaflets, all advertising the same sorts of things and a weird smell was coming off the walls and the floor, kind of clinically disinfected. I waited, half-reading the leaflet titles, half-watching my mum as she peered impatiently into the reception area, her arms folded tightly across her sweater.

A different woman appeared at the window, brown hair in a tight perm and a pair of glasses perched on the end of her nose. 'Come through,' she said to Mum, pointing at a door to the left of the desk.

'Michael,' Mum snapped at me.

The other side of the door the woman was waiting for us. Her back straight and her heels clicking, she walked us through to a dark little room with a single long, thin window at the top of one wall. The florescent lights over us buzzed into action when she flicked the switch.

'Take a seat, Mrs—'

'Hughes,' Mum said.

The woman shuffled round the desk, smoothed the back of her tight brown skirt and sat down, holding her hand out to the two chairs in front of us as she did. We sat.

'Right, Mrs Hughes, what can I do for you?'

'Take him off me,' Mum said, 'I don't want him any more.'

I stared at her, the woman stared at her and no one said anything. I couldn't quite believe that Shirley had brought me here to get rid of me. She had a sadness in her eyes, what might have been the beginnings of tears, yet she was telling a complete stranger to take me away. I was totally confused. If she was mad at me for something, why didn't she just tell me and kick me out for a few nights?

'Seriously,' Shirley said, as if no one had heard her. 'I don't want him, take him away.'

The woman cleared her throat. 'I see,' she said, and she stood up, her hands resting on the table. 'I'll be right back.' She scooted round the table and clicked out of the room.

Shirley continued to stare ahead of her, like she was scrutinising the magnolia paint job on the woodchip wallpaper that lined the office.

I wondered if this was all Frank's idea: he tried physical violence and that didn't work. He tried mental abuse and that didn't work. So now he was making her get rid of me, the ultimate victory, the solution that couldn't fail. Or maybe it was her idea, it's not like she'd ever been motherly and maybe she'd had enough of my attitude. I tried to look at anything that wasn't her: the filing cabinet, a weird spidery plant, a stack of papers, the computer, some big files, the desk, the greying carpet tiles. We waited in silence, and waited and waited. But still the woman didn't return.

Eventually, Shirley spoke: 'They're doing this on purpose, you know. They're trying to make me change my mind.'

We stayed in our chairs for a few more minutes, the bristly fabric starting to itch through my school trousers. Then Shirley grabbed her bag from where she'd dropped it under her chair.

'They're clearly not coming back,' she said. 'I've had enough. I'm leaving.' She stood and walked out of the room. The door pulled itself to and the latch clicked shut behind her.

Everything was silent. Not a sound, from outside or in the rest of Hilden House.

No birds singing, no clock ticking, no phones ringing, no people chatting.

I had a choice: stay, and be taken into care by social services, or run.

I ran.

The receptionist shouted something as I skirted through the door next to her desk, but I didn't hesitate, I just kept on going until I was a couple of hundred feet from Hilden House.

No one was following me. I could see Shirley walking quickly up the street ahead, back towards the bus station, so I crossed the road and slowed my pace. There was no way I was going back with her, knowing she didn't want me, no way I would beg her to take me with her. I'd rather be homeless. Besides, I would be fine on my own, I always was, and I had plenty of mates to help me out.

11

SAFETY IN NUMBERS

Dr Greenberg: *There may be things that you enjoy doing by yourself, but do you usually have more fun when you do things with other people?*

Mark Farina's bedroom light was on as I walked through Padgate later that night. I knocked on the door and a rumbling noise came from inside, of Mark jogging down the stairs. He wasn't being quiet, so I knew his mum wasn't in.

'Alright, mate,' he said, pulling the door open, a big grin on his face.

We sat in his bedroom with huge chunks of bread smothered in peanut butter, playing on his Atari.

He handed me cigarette after cigarette and by the time we went to bed – top and tailing in his single – I was feeling queasy from the smoke. As homelessness goes, this wasn't a bad first night, not that I mentioned the situation to him. There was no need.

The next day, I went to school as normal. In fact, I

continued to go to school most days throughout the time I was homeless. For one thing, because Shirley was on benefits, I got a food token each morning from my form tutor, Mr Hodges, so I got fed every day at school. At night, I would stay with whoever I'd been hanging around with that evening, usually Craig, top and tailing in his bed.

One morning, I woke up to Craig's mum battering me round the head. All of us boys were supposed to be out on the field camping and so Sandra had said Nina, Craig's eldest sister, could sleep in Craig and Nick's room for the night. We'd got freezing cold around three o'clock and had quietly climbed up to the lads' window, so as not to disturb their sleeping parents, telling Nina to get back to her own room. But, when Sandra came to wake Nina in the morning, all she saw was my head sticking out the bottom of the covers, and another body next to me, under the covers. I sat up to say good morning and Sandra's fist met my face. She clipped me round the head several times before Craig unpeeled the duvet from over him and, with his hair stuck on end and his eyes squinting, he said: 'What you doing, Mammy?' To which she jumped back in surprise.

Sandra and Vince always had a house full, so me being there didn't usually make much difference to them. But there came a time, after several months, that my constant presence at tea and bedtime round my closest friends' houses was starting to be very obvious, as was the fact that I was eating all their food. It got harder and harder to stay over, and I still didn't want anyone to know I'd left home, so I decided to take some time off from my network.

The first night I slept out on the streets on my own, I thought it would be a good idea to sleep in a telephone box, just outside Orford Park. It was about midnight that I left Craig's and I wandered around for a while. The warm glow of the light in the phone box lured me in, a safer option than sleeping out in the open. I tucked myself up off the cold ground using some blankets I'd found and my school bag as a pillow. It was late summer and not too chilly out. I actually felt nice and warm as I prepared to get to sleep. But, as I closed my eyes, I heard loud voices approaching from the other end of the street. They were all male voices and obviously drunk, slurring at each other, jeering and laughing loudly. The voices got closer and, just as I thought they hadn't noticed me and were moving on, one man stopped.

'Will you look at this!' he shouted, pointing down at me, lit up as I was by the phone box light. Four other blokes joined him, not much more than silhouettes in the dark, all staring at me huddled in my blankets.

The one who stopped first opened the door. 'I'm busting for a piss, no better place than a phone box, hey, lads?' He unzipped his fly and pulled out his cock, clutching it between two fingers and aiming it straight at me.

I grabbed my blankets and bag off the ground and jumped to my feet, barging past the men just before the guy's stream hit me. Their laughter rocketed into the air as fast as I legged it away, running through the big gates and into Orford Park.

It was dark, but not as frightening as I imagined it would be. At least there weren't any drunken blokes around. I knew there was a hut next to the bowling green, so I jogged across the park and over to it, to see if it was open.

The hut was a bright green tin building and, in the bright moonlight, I could see a huge padlock shining around the door latch. I walked round the side and came across a smaller brick building: the toilet block. The big steel door had a similar padlock and I realised how stupid it was to even have thought it might be open at night. But at least the block was well out of sight of the road. I edged round the corner, to see if there was any shelter at the back, and walked straight into a group of four men: two sitting on the ground, leaning against the side of the block, one sitting on a low brick wall, and one cross-legged on the tarmac between them. I stopped still, cursing under my breath, knowing there was no way I would have gone over if I'd known they were there.

'What do you want?' one of the men against the wall asked me, shaggy dark hair falling into his eyes. He had big Doc Marten boots on and a long overcoat. His face thin and eyes tired.

'Nothing,' I said.

'He wants *nothing*,' the guy next to him drawled. 'So what you doing staring then?'

'I'm not,' I said, full of bravado, but bricking it inside.

'He's *n-n-n-not*,' the first one mimicked, inventing a stutter for me.

'Leave him alone, Jez, he's only a kid.' The one on the low brick wall waved a hand in the direction of the shaggy-haired guy, before turning to me. 'What you doing out on your own this time of night, lad?' he asked, a Liverpool twang in his voice.

I took a punt: 'I'm homeless.'

'Are you now?' He ran a tanned, bony hand through his hair, the mousy strands all sticking together. 'You don't look very homeless.'

I shrugged. 'I've been staying at some mates' houses.'

'What's your name then, kid?'

'Mike.'

'Welcome, Mike, to our humble abode. Grab a seat next to Mouse there and join us.'

Mouse shuffled across the tarmac, making room for me at the friendly guy's feet.

His black leather shoes had as many holes in as mine.

'I'm Baz,' the guy on the wall continued, gesturing with his hand as he spoke, 'this is Mouse, as you already know, and Jez, and Steve.'

I sat down. Mouse nodded his bent head, but didn't glance up. He rolled some flecks of gravel between his fingers, his nails edged with black dirt. Jez and Steve leered at me.

'Why you homeless then, Mike?' Baz started up again, cheerful as hell.

'Mum kicked me out.'

'Well, isn't that a drag. Care for a smoke, my friend?' He produced a packet of backy from inside his green overcoat and handed it to me.

I pulled my blankets around my shoulders and

rolled a cigarette, careful not to use too much of his tobacco so that I was left basically smoking paper.

'Good, good,' Baz said, taking a sip from a bottle of water that lay by his feet. He rolled himself a smoke and asked me question after question, about where I was from, who I knew, what school I went to. Then he started telling me about his school days. He was only twenty or so now, but he talked of them like they were the good old days, long ago, like Grandad used to talk about the war.

Every so often, as he talked, Steve and Jez would make a comment about me getting off now, or they'd start throwing little stones at me that they'd dug out of the tarmac, laughing if they caught me on the head. Baz told them to pack it in, and to shut up, and then went right on reminiscing, like he and I were old friends, and they slumped against each other, quiet again. Baz sounded pretty intelligent when he talked, and he didn't look too shabby either, despite being on the thin side.

After his reminiscing had drawn to a natural conclusion he said: 'Mike, now that we are all friends, and it's getting very late, perhaps you would like to enjoy some of our finest delights?' He held out his hand. In his palm was a small foil package, which he unfolded and carefully, so lightly, lay down in front of him to reveal a small mound of light brown powder. He sank off the low wall to sit on the ground.

Steve and Jez sat upright, and even Mouse lifted his head, stretched his back and legs, as Baz pulled a needle, teaspoon and lighter from a pocket. A couple of long strips of material came out of another pocket. That coat was heroin's answer to Mary Poppins' handbag.

'What do you say?' Baz asked, glancing at me as he gently urged the powder from the foil into the teaspoon. He took up his bottle of water, sucked a small amount out with his syringe and squirted it over the smack. Then he started to heat the concoction with his lighter.

I watched it melt from powder into a sludgy brown liquid.

'I'm alright, but thanks anyway,' I said.

'Doesn't know what he's missing,' Jez said, pulling his own foil package from inside his boot.

Baz placed a grubby, balled up bit of cotton wool into the liquid then dipped his needle in and drew up the scag. He held the needle up in the moonlight, flicking it to displace any air, clenched the syringe between his teeth and slid his jacket off. I half turned my head, pretending to be interested in something else in the park, but watched him carefully from the corner of my eye.

Track marks with scabs and purpled bruises dotted his inner arm. He tied one of the blue strips of material around his bicep – one end hanging free, the other he placed between his teeth, taking the syringe back in his hand. He pulled the tourniquet tight and drew the needle up to his skin, pressing it gently into the flesh. Slowly, he took in a breath and pushed down; the heroin slipped into his vein, his eyes closed and his head tilted back to the sky. The needle hung there for a moment, his fingers limply supporting it, before he removed it and let out his held breath. Mouse took the spoon from by Baz's feet and set about heating the smack up again. He reached for

Baz's needle to draw it out. Jez and Steve were cooking up their own batch in another spoon.

Baz was staring at the sky, grinning, looking purely happy. But not one bit of me was tempted. I couldn't understand how someone with intelligence would ever try heroin: everyone knows how incredibly addictive the stuff is, and how it never ends well. The Rastas I used to hang around with in the café with Pete Richards, back in Manchester, would tell us about the smack-heads they'd come across. It always, inevitably, ended in overdose because no one ever knew what the stuff was cut with.

That, or prison, because they'd be desperate for money and go nicking off anyone in broad daylight. It made no sense to me why you'd try it even once.

'Beautiful, just beautiful,' Baz said. 'The way the moonlight dances on the grass.'

'Baz–' his glazed eyes made me more sure of myself '–how's it feel?'

'It feels like…' He paused to consider, like he was desperate to give me the right answer and anything else just wouldn't do. 'It feels like sex,' he began. 'You're too young to know, but man, when you're older you will. It's that release you get from coming, when you're inside a girl – deep, deep inside her – and you've been pumping away and building up and building up and up and up and then, wham, you can't hold it off for one more second and it all comes shooting out and you feel it through every inch of your body, in your veins. That. That's how it feels. But ten times better. Fuckin' amazing.' And he laughed a deep, belly laugh.

Steve, Jez and Mouse were all alert now and they joined in the laughter, agreeing with Baz, telling him he was 'poetic'. We all got talking, them gibbering on about stuff, and me nodding and agreeing. Then, one by one, they passed into a smack-induced sleep.

I sat there in my blankets watching them slowly breathe, listening to sirens in the distance and leaves rustling in the trees. I shuffled closer to Baz, leaning against the low wall next to him, and tried closing my eyes, wishing for sleep, but it only came in bursts. Seeing Baz passed out, I still didn't get it, why he ever tried the stuff in the first place – it was such a waste of an intelligent person. He was an unconscious mess. Safety in numbers, I kept thinking, every time I glanced down at their discarded needles.

*

Hours later, the guys woke up and gathered their stuff together. It was about 6am.

'Pleasure to meet you, Michael,' Baz said, pulling on his coat and grinning at me again. 'I'm off to get me bag for the day.' They walked off as a pack, leaving me alone with the sounds of the park.

I shrugged off my blankets and stashed them in my school bag, then headed over to Padgate. For once, I was the first person in school. The caretaker opened the gates – saying to me, 'You're keen' – and in I went, straight to the lads' toilet to relieve myself. I stripped off my dirty clothes, washed all over, got dressed again and headed over to my form room. None of my mates or Mr Hodges guessed how I'd spent the night, no one questioned my appearance. That was the useful thing about being poor: I didn't look that different now that I was sleeping rough. It wasn't unusual for my clothes not to be washed, or for me to be a bit tired.

Over the next two months I continued sleeping at Baz and his mates' spot by the bowling green hut. Some nights I tried going off on my own, not wanting to watch them shoot up yet again, and I attempted sleeping under trees in various parks. But, if you've ever tried it, you'll know how hard it is to get to sleep under a tree.

Eventually, I'd go back to the hut and find them gathered there. Safety in numbers, I kept telling myself.

To keep sweet with them, I always talked to Baz about the stuff he was interested in, knowing that if he liked having me around, the others wouldn't care so much. I asked him questions about the heroin, more about how it felt and how he got it. He told me how every morning they'd wake up and immediately start trying to find money. They had to beg, borrow and steal to get enough together. Sometimes they'd get the heroin 'on tick', as Baz called it – owing the dealer, telling him they were good for it, but that was a dangerous game, he said. We'd talk about other things too, like I said, Baz was really clever. He knew all about computers and how they worked and loved telling me intricate details of their make up. But the conversations only ever lasted an hour or two before they'd all be craving their next hit.

Weekends were the hardest thing to cope with. I didn't want to see my mates, still trying to give them enough of a break of me, so that I could eventually start staying round theirs again. Waking up in a park with a load of smack-heads deserting you, their mission for the day focussed and obvious, when you have nothing, literally nothing to do, is hard. I would consider going into town, but would know I had to get through two days without food and that the walk would exhaust me too quickly. I never crave food – I think that has something to do with the anhedonia and not getting any enjoyment from food whatsoever – but I do feel weak after a while of not eating.

First thing in the morning I'd hunt out a construction site so I could go take a shit in a place where no one could see. A pretty awful present for the poor builders on Monday morning, but something I had to do. If I had underwear on, I'd use it to get clean. If I didn't, I'd try and find some bits of rag or newspaper on my walk to the building site that I could use. Then I'd just wander the area I was in, sit in the park, wait for time to pass. I knew, very clearly, that there was no purpose to my life.

This is where I feel lucky to have anhedonia. At least, as lucky as I can feel.

Because, without it, I'm not sure I'd have coped with being homeless and having nothing to live for. I got it into my head that I just had to wait the weekend out and that, on Monday, I'd be able to go to school and get cleaned up. I'd learn stuff and see my mates. I might go round Mark's house after school for an hour or two, or we might play five-aside, or Andrew's mum might offer to wash my clothes. 'Go on, strip off, I'll throw your uniform in too,' she'd say and I'd stand there in something of Andrew's until everything was dry. All I had to do was make it through the weekend, then I'd have a purpose again.

12

LISA

Dr Greenberg: Would you agree that sex is okay, but not as much fun as people claim it is?

Lisa was in my year at school and a total rock chick. Long black hair, a black t-shirt with the sleeves rolled up and rips down the side, black jeans with DMs, and thick black pencil lining her eyes. Her appearance screamed that she didn't care; that she was a rebel. And I adored her. To begin, it was one of my flickers: lust.

The first time she ever spoke to me, I was convinced that she was going to flutter her eyes and wait for me to ask her out.

We were at school: I was with the lads at break time; she was with her group of girls across the field. As I saw her coming towards me, her dark eyes fixed on mine, and I knew this was it, my time to shine.

'Alright, Mike,' she said, those thick black lashes fluttering. 'I wanted to ask you something.'

'Yes?' I said, getting ready to snog her face off.

'My friend Caroline really likes you, will you go out with her?'

I focussed on the group of girls behind her. Sure enough, blonde-haired, athletic little Caroline was surrounded by the others, sheepishly smiling at me.

'But it's you I like,' I said to Lisa, not quite believing that she was turning me down before I'd even asked her out.

'Well, go out with her for me then, will you? She really, really likes you. It would mean a lot to me.'

'I dunno. She's not my type.'

Lisa put her hand on my arm. Her nails were short and painted black.

'Fine,' I said. 'I'll go out with her if that's what you want.'

Immediately, Lisa turned and jogged over to the girls. I heard her say: 'He wants to go out with you!' to Caroline, and Caroline came sauntering over, giggling and twiddling the ends of her ponytail between her fingers.

She stood in front of me. 'Well?' she said, when I just stared at her, her voice as little as she was.

I shuffled on the spot, feeling trapped. 'Lisa said I should ask you out.'

She flung her arms around my waist, her head resting on my chest. 'I will!'

After that fateful afternoon, Caroline never left my side. She was always all over me – no other girl would come near now that I was Caroline's 'boyfriend', she was a feisty little thing and scared just about anyone who crossed her path, male or female – no matter what I did, I couldn't get away. I'd go and play five-aside with the boys, and Caroline would be there; I'd go over to Craig's to hang out, and Caroline would be there; I'd go to a party and Caroline would be there; it became easier to just go where Caroline went. And that often meant a trip to Lisa's.

Lisa's dad was a local minister and for some reason he was never home, off seeing to his parishioners, or something. Her mum wasn't on the scene at all, so her house was pretty much a free-for-all and a place where everyone in our circle began to hang out.

Sometimes, I'd think that Lisa and I might have a chance, despite Caroline. If Caroline was busy with family stuff, I'd automatically go to see what was happening at Lisa's. We'd often get close on her sofa and she'd rest her hands on my legs. One time we were alone in the house and Lisa dragged me upstairs to her bedroom, but instead of throwing me on the bed and ravishing me like I'd been imagining, she shoved me into her wardrobe and, moments later, her dad walked in. After he'd gone, she said I'd better leave. I don't think I ever gave up hope that she and I might one day get together. Although the lust thing quickly subsided – like it always does with me – I realised that being around her was better than being around anyone else I knew. She was kind and caring, attentive. Time with her was easy.

It wasn't like that with obsessive, possessive little Caroline. What I did get from Caroline, though, was worth more than a relationship with Lisa – on a practical level.

As soon as we started seeing each other, Caroline began taking me along to hers for tea every night, and her parents, Neville and Jane, welcomed me to their table. They were a good Christian couple who had adopted both Caroline and her younger brother, Eric, from separate families. Another mouth to feed was another good deed, in their eyes. Caroline's birth mum had been a prostitute, which maybe explained Caroline's overly physical nature with me, and she had no idea who her dad was – it was amazing how much we actually had in common, though we didn't know it at the time.

I'd been sleeping rough for almost two months when Caroline and I got together. After just a couple of weeks of going round to hers after school every night for tea, and staying late in the evening, Neville and Jane worked out what no one else had: I was homeless. They called me into the kitchen to talk to me.

Caroline and I sat side by side, her parents across from us at their big pine table, their dog – a floppy-eared spaniel, called Sandy – curled up on my feet below. Eric had been sent to his room. Caroline's hand, as it always did when we sat next to each other, was creeping up my thigh, hidden by the folds of the floral tablecloth.

Jane cleared her throat and her mousey, permed hair ruffled with the movement. She was a short, curvy woman, a bit posher than anyone else I knew, and she always spoke in a considered way.

'Michael,' she started, 'we've noticed you seem to like it here.'

Here we go, I thought, the big kick-out story. She knew how to be diplomatic, at least: I'd spent every single evening there, eating their food and watching their TV. I nodded, avoiding her eye contact, and instead watched Neville pull his pipe from his jacket pocket and begin compacting tobacco into its bowl. He was the opposite of Jane, long and thin and with strawberry-blonde hair that sat in curls on top of his narrow head. He worked at Crosfield's, where they made soap powder, and must have had a fairly decent job as they were rich, at least by my standards – living in a semi, owning a car and having regular holidays was a hell of a lot more than other people I knew.

'And we like having you,' Jane went on. That was unexpected.

Neville continued to concentrate on his pipe. Caroline squeezed my leg, in agreement with her mother's words.

'If you would like – and, of course, if Caroline agrees – you are very welcome to stay with us for a while. You may have a sleeping bag and can sleep on Caroline's floor.'

'I agree!' Caroline's hand felt like it was going to squeeze through my flesh into the bone with the strength she was gripping it, excitement pulsing through her. I stole a quick look at her face and saw, externally, she was as calm and collected as was appropriate, a meek smile on her face.

I considered what Jane was suggesting. I didn't want to be with Caroline and was only doing it because Lisa had asked me to. Besides, I liked my independence and living with them would stop me from doing what I wanted when I wanted. But I was still sleeping rough most nights and, though I was sure my mates would put me up again after all this time, I knew there'd come a point where it got too much for them once more. That empty feeling of no purpose was hovering over me like a threat. Here, Jane and Neville would feed me, probably clothe me, maybe even give me pocket money for doing chores, like they did with Caroline and Eric. It seemed a sensible option, whether I wanted to be with Caroline or not; had I been with Lisa, there was no way her dad would have allowed me to move in, I'm sure.

'Okay,' I said, and that was that.

Neville lit his pipe and Jane, smiling, stood to do the washing up. Caroline grabbed my hand and virtually pulled me out of my chair. She dragged me upstairs, sat me on the bed and started ramming her tongue down my throat. I sat there and let her do what she wanted. At least there was a more practical reason for our relationship now.

*

Caroline was an insatiable girl. We were still so young, but she opened my eyes to so many new things. After I'd been living at her place for a little while, her parents took me away on holiday with them to Wales. We all stayed in a caravan and spent days walking around various sights. On the final day, Caroline and I went off for a walk around the campsite and ended up on top of a deserted hill, looking down on where we were staying. It was there that I lost my virginity.

Having anhedonia means it's near impossible to experience pleasure. And for me, as a teenager, that was definitely the case. But, like all straight boys, I still got physically aroused at the sight of a naked female body, and I even found something in masturbation that pleased me. It was a physical sensation that I hadn't experienced before, something different, and that release was definitely something good, not bad. Having sex was even better: getting a girl to do it all for me and for me to still feel the same physical sensations was ace. But it didn't take a lot for me to lose interest in sex. Caroline wanted it all the time, which was easy as I was staying in her room – her parents were utterly clueless about their daughter's urges – but once I'd got over the initial novelty of having sex, I had no appetite for it, just going along with it when I felt I could to save hurting her feelings. I've always been quite intuitive, at least.

In school, she was a good girl, getting on with her work fastidiously, and this made me follow suit. I regularly attended classes now, not wanting to rock the boat with Neville and Jane who placed a lot of stock into school achievements, though I still didn't see the point in doing my homework; when Caroline was studying at home, I'd be out with my mates – or at Lisa's. Caroline also attended all the church events her parents helped organise, from garden fêtes to carol concerts. Luckily, they never told me to go to these things. Out of school and church, though, Caroline wasn't the same angelic little girl she portrayed. She smoked with the best of them, saving the dinner money Neville gave her each morning to buy packets of Bensons. Whenever the rest of the family went on holiday, she threw massive house parties that were well renowned amongst our friends. And later I discovered that even before me she'd been promiscuous with the boys – earning herself the nickname banana girl for a sex act she performed for several of the boys, me not included.

The years that I lived under Neville and Jane's roof were the most stable of my childhood. They cared for me almost as though I was another adopted son. Every night after school we'd all sit around the kitchen table for tea that Jane had cooked up.

They'd buy me clothes and shoes and make sure I had all I needed for school: pens, books, scientific calculators and all that.

Caroline and Eric were bought far more than I was, but that suited me fine, I didn't want much. And I definitely didn't want to be thought of as part of the family, because I didn't need a family. To make that distinction clear, whenever Christmas came around I'd make up some excuse that they couldn't protest against – 'Mum's asked me to go round hers', or 'I'm off to me nan and grandad's this year' – in order to avoid it. Instead, I'd see if any mates were hanging around or I'd go and sit in a park, waiting for it all to be over. They'd still buy me a gift though, leaving it on my sleeping bag in Caroline's room.

The shame is that I didn't appreciate all that Jane and Neville did. It's only as an adult that I see how far they went out of their way for me. No matter what I did – I smashed the glass in their front door by shutting it too hard, and shattered an expensive glass lampshade with my head because I jumped too high when I was showing Eric how to do a karate kick – they didn't shout or scream, or even get angry, all they were bothered about was whether I'd hurt myself. I knew they were good Christian folk and I figured they got some kind of kick out of helping me, duty-bound as their religion made them. I wasn't rude to them – not like I had been with Shirley – but I didn't show gratitude for all their efforts, because that's not something I felt. They were a means to an end and I took all that they had to offer, knowing I was in a decent position and wondering when it would all end.

*

The end finally came because I couldn't take being with Caroline any longer. I was sixteen and had been living there for three years, and in all that time she rarely left my side. By then, I'd lost touch a bit with Craig, Andrew and Mark, because I was always doing what Caroline wanted to do, and so I began hanging out with them again. There was no big break-up between Caroline and I, more of a fizzle. I started staying the odd night at the lads' houses and slowly went there more and more and spent time with Caroline less and less, until I just stopped going round to hers. Neville and Jane never said anything about my absence, they probably felt a relief.

In the few months between my sixteenth birthday and my O Level exams that summer, I dossed between Andrew, Craig and Mark's houses, top and tailing with each of them again and getting fed where I could. I sat my O Levels without much care – without crucial things like pens and calculators; a pencil I found on the ground outside the exam room got me through – and I came out with decent enough grades in English language and literature, French, maths and computer studies. Those were the useful subjects and they all came naturally to me; I never saw much point in the other subjects and have no idea how I did in them. My O Level certificates must have been delivered to Shirley's that summer, but I never went to get them. Throughout my life, qualifications haven't meant anything to me. I don't mind learning something new, but having a certificate to tell the world I'm good at that thing seems a waste of paper.

13

KNOWING CRAIG

Dr Greenberg: Are there many pursuits that you can say you have ever really enjoyed doing?

As soon as the exams were over – and me and the lads had a week or two to celebrate finishing school forever – I signed up to the Youth Training Scheme (YTS). It was a government scheme that provided funded training and it paid a wage. Warrington Information Technology Centre took me on and I learnt everything from reception work, to word processing and even computer programming. It felt useful and like I was doing something worthwhile, better than school, plus the Lion across the road was a great place for dinner and a pint every lunch.

Everyone knew, by that point, that if I wasn't living with Caroline I was homeless, so Craig's mum and dad invited me to move into theirs. I paid thirty pounds a week rent – half my wages – and slept on the lower bunk of Nick's bed, with Craig across from us in his newly bought single. It was a proper arrangement, finally, and it felt better that I was paying my way.

We all worked hard then – Nick doing the doors in the local roller rink, Craig in the abattoir, coming home stinking of meat, Mark as a sales assistant in an electronics shop, and Andrew first helping on the milk round, then later working with Caroline's dad at Crosfield's Soap Works (Caroline had started dating him soon after she and I broke up, trying to get back at me) – but at weekends we'd be down the social club, playing pool and drinking till we couldn't stand up. We all had skinheads and we got ourselves some tattoos: a grim reaper for me, a snake for Craig. Generally speaking, we had a laugh spending our hard-earned cash.

For a while, I felt like the richest guy around and I'd buy drinks for everyone all the time. To get paid from the YTS I had to have a bank account and with that I received a cheque book. They told me that if I wanted money all I had to do was make a cheque out to 'cash', so day after day I would write cheques for thirty quid, over and over. At the start, I thought my pay packet was going a long way, but when it carried on and no one stopped me I realised I was getting away with something. I thought, *Why not?* and carried on. After a few weeks, though, the bank realised what was happening and put a freeze on my account, insisting I pay it all back and leaving me with a load of debt. Not that the debt fazed me, because nothing could.

Around that time I tried another scam, this one a bit more serious. The accountant at work, Matthew Bluden, was a nice guy, a bit dorky with his side-parted hair and glasses, but decent enough. At one point I had the job of getting him to sign various documents – containing information about him, like his date of birth, home address and bank details. When he signed, I noticed that his signature was an incredibly simple one.

Without thinking too much about it, in my split-second way, I decided to see if I could get a little extra cash by impersonating him. I went along to TSB in Penketh, on the outskirts of Warrington, and when the clerk came over to me I asked her if I could get an account balance, please.

'Yes, of course,' the girl said, her smile as shining as her name badge that told me she was called Michelle. 'If you could just write your name and address down for me.'

She slid a piece of paper towards me and I wrote Matthew's details down. The next slip of paper she produced was the balance: £601.

I'd practiced my lines: 'I'm in a bit of a quandary and I wonder if there's a way you can help me, Michelle. You see, I'm about to buy a car off someone but I don't have any cheques left in my book. Is there anything you can do?'

'Of course, sir,' Michelle smiled, looking especially pleased with herself for knowing the answer to my problem. 'We can write you a banker's cheque.'

'Wonderful,' I said. And off she went.

She came back with the cheque, asked me to sign it – which I did perfectly – and to write down my date of birth, then she checked what I'd done and asked whether I'd like it in tens or twenties.

'Twenties,' I replied, amazed it had worked.

Because it was so easy, I decided to try again, with another work colleague, Stephen Borsey, who banked at Barclays (I wasn't going to try it again at TSB). I went into the branch and repeated exactly what I'd done the first time. Need my account balance, trying to buy a car, banker's cheque, *oh yes, please*. When the clerk produced the banker's cheque for me to sign and asked for my date of birth, I realised I couldn't remember Stephen's birth date. I racked my brains. Was it the fourteenth or fifteenth of May? I took a gamble and wrote down the fifteenth.

The clerk took the paper from me and inspected my signature and the date. I watched her eyes narrow as she scrutinized the paper.

'Just a moment,' she said, pushing herself off her chair. She strolled over to a desk at the back of the office where a balding man sat at a computer. She bent her head to his and spoke quietly to him. As the words came out, her eyes darted up to look at me, and his gaze followed hers, moving between me and the cheque in front of him.

I turned and ran.

I ran out of the bank and down the street, along the road and up to the park. I glanced back over my shoulder and saw a group of men in suits spilling out of the bank doors, all hot and bothered, looking this way and that to see if they could spot the fraudulent culprit. But I was long gone and blending well into the people milling along the street.

I may not have any emotional recognition, but I know when I'm on a dangerous path and I vowed never to try that again. That night, though, I told the lads about my afternoon escapade and they laughed along, clapping me on the back and agreeing how close a shave it was.

We were young lads having a good time and inevitably we all got up to a bit of mischief, each in our own way. We were inclined to have a bit of fun together as well.

One Saturday night, around midnight, we were round Mark's when Craig suggested we break into the local Spar shop. It was the place everyone robbed in our area and more a rite of passage than a heinous crime. Just as everyone before us had done, Craig, Mark and I all climbed onto the flat roof of the Spar shop and Craig levered open the plastic skylight with a crowbar he'd brought along. Mark went in first, gripping onto the metal edge of the skylight and swinging himself down to the shelf below. A lot of rustling followed his movements, then a couple of dense thuds. I stuck my head down into the dark shop, shining my torch around. Mark was collapsed on the floor of the shop, crisp packets all around him, laughing his head off. I quickly jumped down after him, onto the now-clear shelf, and Craig followed.

Once inside, Craig and Mark grabbed a couple of trolleys and ran around the aisles piling loads of stuff in. They sang 'Bat Out of Hell' at the top of their voices, scooping up boxes of cereal, tubs of ice cream, even washing powder and tins of soup, before getting to the alcohol section. They grabbed a few crates of lager and a couple of bottles of cider and threw those in too.

Leaning against the counter, I watched them for a

few minutes, before butting in.

'Lads, how are you planning on getting all that crap out the skylight?'

The door to the shop had several sturdy locks to prevent thieves from breaking in, and, I guess, from getting out. And there was no way we were getting all that up and out the skylight. How would we carry it even if we got it out?

I grabbed a few boxes of cigarettes for us all and joined them at their trolleys. We each took a crate of lager and pushed the trolleys as hard as we could to the other end of the shop, smashing them into the doors of the freezers.

Wading through crisp packets, we heaved ourselves up onto the shelves again and Craig, ever the strong man, climbed out onto the roof first so we could pass up the three crates of lager. He held out an arm and I pulled myself up after him, soon followed by Mark. The only thing left to do now we were out with our loot was to drink it.

We headed over to the school, a short walk away, and settled down on the generator box by one of the English classrooms, cracking our cans open. For a couple of hours we drank can, after can, after can and told stories, shouted at the tops of our voices and took the piss out of each other.

At one point, Mark stood up and started singing the national anthem. He flung his arms around like a windmill and turned in circles as he went on. Just as he threw his arms out in an emotional finale, his hand flailed much too far and too vigorously behind him, hit the window and shattered the glass.

'Fuck!' Craig and I both shouted.

'You knob!' Craig said, creasing over in laughter as Mark held his hand out, blood starting to drip from his knuckles.

Mark danced around for a minute in pain, clutching his hand to him, pressing it to his t-shirt to stop the bleeding.

'I have an idea…' Craig jumped up, kicking his can of beer over, and with his shirt sleeve covering his hand he brushed away the broken glass from the window ledge.

'An open window is the perfect invitation! Come on,' he said, climbing into the hall.

We ran around the school like maniacs, larking about, throwing blackboard dusters at each other, grabbing TVs out of the English rooms and throwing them as far as we could down the corridors, like we were bowling. We tore into the headmaster's office – a new bloke we didn't even know – and threw all his papers around, pulling them out of drawers and filing cabinets and prancing about in them. We turned all the gas taps on in the science lab and, as we left, started flicking lit matches down the long corridor, back towards the lab. God knows what we'd have done if they'd caught – gone up with the whole building no doubt.

That was one of our more crazy evenings; they weren't all like that. Mostly, we drank down the pub, or in the park, or round one of our houses. It was a simple time without much going on to bother anyone. By May, Craig had saved up enough to rent a bedsit behind a local club and so he moved out, leaving

Nick and me with a bit more space. Now and again, Caroline would turn up at the house asking for me. But everyone – even Vince and Sandra – was well versed in telling her I wasn't there, especially when I was. If she had one of her house parties, or if the lads decided to hang out round hers, I would go along and she would, inevitably, try it on with me.

Sometimes I'd reject her flat out – say, 'No, you're supposed to be with Andrew now' – and walk away, but then she'd cry. Other times I'd give in, just to avoid the drama. Generally, I tried to avoid her as best I could. Other than that, it was a pretty easy life.

Before I knew it, a year had passed and my training with the YTS was almost over. I had two choices for the end of the summer: one, do a second year there, or two get a bigger, better job with more money. I didn't really know what to do with myself, but on my way to work one Wednesday at the end of June I bumped into an army recruitment guy in the street. He sold it to me pretty well – a life in the army – and in my usual style, I decided on the spot that this was what I should do. I made an appointment and two weeks later went along on a Monday afternoon after work to sit the test paper the army give everyone to find out if you're suitable enough.

Inside the Winmarleigh Street building, I squirmed in my smart shirt and jeans, the army officers surrounding me all crisp and starched. They looked like they had a purpose to their days, which seemed a fairly good idea to someone like me who had no purpose and no feeling. A guy with an immaculately trimmed moustache sat behind a desk with clipboards and forms in front of him. I told him my name and he ticked me off on a list of about twenty, then handed me a board with the test paper attached.

'Through there.' He gestured with his hand to double doors. 'Choose a seat and begin. There are pens on the desks. You have an hour and a half, no more.'

I had no idea what to expect, but as I sat down and scanned through the questions I realised there were indentations all over the paper. Every question had been answered already, but rubbed out. I read through the first lot of questions – all on problem solving, how to get a pulley to turn a cog if it's set up in such and such a way – and as far as I could see, the rubbed out answers seemed to be right. Taking a punt that this was a paper one of the officers had used for something, I followed the marks and filled it out verbatim. Within forty minutes, I'd finished the lot, got up and handed my complete paper in to the man with the perfect moustache.

'Finished already? Have a seat over there.'

Scepticism covered his face as he began checking off the answers. But by the time he reached the end, he got straight to his feet and came out from behind his desk, his hand outstretched.

'Hughes, I'm impressed,' he said, shaking my hand. 'I didn't think it to look at you, but you got one hundred percent, and in one of the fastest times I think we've ever had. You'll be accepted for pretty much any job in the army with that score. Well done.'

*

That Wednesday Craig met me from work and we walked down towards the social club. He hadn't been home yet for a shower and the stench of meat was all over him.

'Not bothering with showers any more then, mate?'

Craig laughed. 'Taking a leaf out of your book, mate. I'm gagging for a pint, couldn't be arsed to go home first.'

'Tough day?'

'It was alright. My back's killing me though. I'm thinking you've got it right joining up, be a damn sight easier than my job, that's for sure.' It was my turn to laugh, so I did, automatically.

'How's all that going, with the army like?'

'It's great. I passed their written test and they've said I can join. On Friday they want me to go down Sutton Coldfield for a physical test.' Craig wolf whistled.

'Not like that.'

'Shame. Could just imagine some blonde little nurse…' He waved his hands, simulating a girl's curves.

'Yeah. Listen, I have got a bit of a problem as it goes. They're asking for me medical card and birth certificate – you know, as proof and whatnot of who I am.'

'Is that right?'

'But they're round Caroline's. My sister brought them round when I first moved in there and Caroline always kept them in her drawer. She's been holding them hostage since we broke up.'

'That girl's fucking nuts, mate.'

'Tell me about it. I could go round, get Jane to

make her give me them, but the whole family's away on one of their holidays. Greece or something. They're not back until next week and the guy down the recruitment office says I need my documents for Friday, else they won't let me in.'

Without a moment's hesitation, Craig gave me a solution: 'We'll go and get them tonight, then.'

'How are we going to get in?'

'Trust me,' Craig said. 'Trust me.'

*

After the pub I went home and got changed; Craig and I had agreed to meet at mine at 10pm. Nick was out and Vince and Sandra had some friends around, drinking a few cans in the back garden, the late evening sun still on them. I grabbed some bread and milk and went up to mine and Nick's room. An array of shirts lay across Nick's bed – he was the vainest bloke I knew, worse than a girl for getting ready. I grabbed a fresh denim shirt and pair of jeans off the floor by my bed and went through to the bathroom to get showered.

All this army stuff felt kind of right. I had a sense of purpose, something to work towards that would be at least a constant for as long as I wanted it. I had no concerns about passing the physical. I may not have been as strong as Craig, lugging meat about on his shoulders all day, but I could still run as fast as when I was a kid. I was lean and fit and able to handle myself in any scenario.

*

I met Craig outside dead on 10pm, just before it got

properly dark. He was waiting for me, leaning against the wall, a fag hanging out his mouth. I sparked one up for the walk and on we went.

We stopped briefly at Mark's, asking if he would like to join us.

'What you going there for, aren't they on holiday?' he said, when we told him we were off to Caroline's.

'Mental cow's holding Mike's birth certificate hostage and he needs it,' Craig said.

'What better time to get it than when we don't have to see her?'

Mark laughed. 'So you're letting yourselves in, are you?'

'That's about the lot of it, yeah,' Craig said. 'Are you coming or just going to stand here chatting about it all night?'

'Can't lads, sorry. I'm taking Jenny out for a night on the town.'

'Going down the social then, I suppose?' I said.

'Yeah, mate.'

'So fucking predictable, Farina.'

Within fifteen minutes of leaving Mark to his date, we arrived at Caroline's. The lights were all out and curtains closed, but every house around theirs was lit up with folk still watching the ten o'clock news on the BBC before bed. I knew that's what they'd be doing, because that's what Neville and Jane would have been doing, had they not been in Greece with Caroline and Eric.

'Quick, get round the back,' Craig said to me,

swiftly moving down the side of Caroline's house.

As we approached the kitchen window, Craig pulled a long stem of wire from inside his jeans.

With one hand he wedged the tips of his fingers under the edge of the window, and with the other he levered the wire in through the gap he'd created between window and frame. Expertly, he twisted the wire through, curled its end round the window latch and raised the latch up off its hook.

I watched in absolute wonder, marvelling at how on earth Craig knew how to do this. I was literally amazed; I never would have thought it was so easy to get into a house.

Craig held the open window aloft for me and we climbed in, stepping across the sink and jumping onto the smooth lino floor with a thud. I left Craig in the kitchen and quietly ran straight up to Caroline's bedroom. Without turning the lights on – conscious that we really shouldn't be in there and worried the neighbours would see us – I carefully rummaged through each of the drawers in Caroline's room. But my documents weren't in there. I searched her desk, lifting every bit of paper and putting each one back in exactly the same place, not wanting her to know I had been going through her stuff. I searched under the mattress, in the chest of drawers, around the hi-fi, even under the rugs, but, despite going over every nook and cranny, I couldn't find where she'd hidden my documents. I hurried back down the stairs.

'They're not here, let's go,' I said in a low voice.

Craig was in the centre of the living room, crouching down, his torch in his mouth shining into a box on the floor.

'What are you doing?' I asked.

'Found a load of stubbies in the garage,' Craig said, standing and holding up a box of French bottled beer like a trophy. 'And this tin with a load of jewellery in it.' He kicked at a rusty old Quality Street tin by his feet then stepped over to the bookshelves by the fireplace. 'Do you mind if I take this hi-fi as well? I really need one for me new flat.'

'What you asking me for? It's nothing to do with me.'

We grabbed some bin bags from under the kitchen sink and I helped Craig put the lager, tin and hi-fi into them. I saw him starting to survey the rest of the stuff in the lounge.

'Let's get out of here,' I said, before he took anything else.

It was completely dark out now and we left through the front door, carrying our bin bags with us. We decided to go straight back to Craig's, to drop the stuff off, and the most direct route was down the train line.

Craig rooted through the Quality Street tin as we walked. He pulled out a few earrings and necklaces, then a gold watch, which he held up to the moonlight, before biting down on the linked strap.

'That's useless, I could put my teeth right through it,' he said and chucked it as hard as he could into the thick brambles next to the train tracks.

'Don't bloody do that,' I said. 'That was Neville's retirement watch.'

'If it was, he was done over, that thing was fake, I'm telling you.' And on he went, rifling through the finds. Oblivious to the fact that he'd just thrown the most valuable thing away – to him and to poor Neville.

'You're an idiot.'

'Check this out.' He held up a brooch and inspected its golden glow, then dropped it back into the tin.

We came off the train line and out by the Asda supermarket, grabbing an abandoned trolley from the car park as we went and chucking the black bags into it to save our arms. I pushed it along the pavement, the wheels wobbling in every direction and Craig gibbering away next to me about some nonsense.

As we came down the slope from Asda, I could see car headlights ahead of us, hovering where they were, shining out from behind a wall. We carried on a bit further. Craig finished sorting and put the Quality Street tin back into the trolley.

Another few paces and the headlights still hadn't moved. I realised what was going on.

'Police!' I shouted to Craig, and just a second after I did the car came out from behind the wall, driving towards us.

Craig ran.

I stopped, my hands still on the trolley. It didn't occur to me to run. I didn't feel like I'd done anything I should run away from: I used to live at the house and knew Neville and Jane wouldn't mind me going in without permission, even if we did take a few things.

The car pulled up beside me and a lanky policeman got out, his hand resting on the truncheon on his belt.

In the streetlight I could see he wasn't much older than me and had pockmarks dimpling his cheeks.

'And what are you doing?' He eyed the trolley and looked me up and down.

'Shopping,' I said, belligerent as ever.

'Funny. Where have you been?'

'Just my ex-girlfriend's.'

'What have you been doing there?'

'Looking for my birth certificate.'

'So what's all this?' He indicated to the stash of black bin bags in the trolley, the top of the hi-fi clearly visible.

'Just some stuff.'

'And where has this "stuff" come from?'

'My ex-girlfriend's.'

I didn't see the need to lie: it was Caroline's stuff and she wouldn't have said anything about me taking it, she was still besotted with me. There was no way Neville and Jane would care either and, if they did, I'd just give it back to them.

'So who's been with you while you were *visiting* your ex-girlfriend's then?'

'No one, I've been on my own.'

'Come on, Mike, don't mess me around.'

I stared at him for a second, surprised that he knew my name. 'I'm not messing you around.'

'We've been watching you and Craig all the way. We know exactly what you've been up to. You're under arrest, for burglary.' The policeman stepped around me and grabbed my hands, starting to place cuffs over my wrists.

'You can't do that, I haven't done anything wrong,' I said. 'This all belongs to my ex. She won't mind, honest.'

'We'll see about that down the station.'

He closed the cuffs tight on my wrists, pinching the skin. 'Mike Hughes, I'm placing you under arrest. You do not have to say anything, but anything you do say may be given as evidence.'

His hand went onto my head and he guided me to the back of the Panda, pushing me down onto the back seat.

*

This police station was bigger than the one Shirley had left me in as a child. At the front desk, I had to tell them my name, age, address and get my fingerprints taken, before they took me into one of twelve holding cells out the back of the station. The heavy door slammed shut behind me.

'We'll be interviewing you shortly,' the young policeman who'd brought me in said.

I sat on the wooden bench at the back of the blank cell, waiting. Within ten minutes, I heard Craig's loud mouth bellowing from the front of the police station.

'Bloody get off me,' he shouted, his voice getting closer to where I was. 'I can walk on me own!'

'Alright, Craig!' I called through my door as his footsteps passed.

'They've got you as well have they?'

'That's enough catching up, you two,' a deep voice said. 'Get in there.' A heavy door banged shut a few cells up from mine.

'Right, out you,' the same voice said.

My door opened. In front of me was a large policeman wearing a flat hat. He was just as tall as the young lad, but with a middle-aged gut. He took me through to a small room that housed just a wooden table, with a tape recorder on top of it and four plastic chairs tucked underneath. The burly policeman told me where to sit, then sat himself across from me placing a pile of headed paper and a pen on the table in front of him.

'George,' he said, leaning back in his chair and directing the comment through the open door. 'Get us a couple of coffees, will you?'

Only a minute or so passed before the policeman with the pocked cheeks strolled through the door, three yellow plastic cups clutched in his hand.

'Sugar?' he asked me. I shook my head.

'You're a lot quieter than your mate, aren't you?' the burly one said, reaching out and flicking the red button on the tape recorder. It whirred into action, the wheels spinning the fine tape slowly round and round.

'We're going to take a statement from you now, Michael. You need to tell us what happened tonight, word for word exactly what you did and when. Whatever you say, we have to write down and it will later be read out in court, so don't start swearing.' He chuckled to himself.

I grinned. 'Ow, ow, ow, stop hitting me, Officer. Stop putting those drugs in my pocket, Officer!'

'Yes, that's very funny,' the burly one said, actually writing down my words as he spoke. 'You might want to take this a little more seriously from here on out. You're in a lot of trouble. Don't think because you're only seventeen that you're going to get off scot-free. Now, start at the beginning. What happened tonight?'

I went through every event, from the moment we left Sandra and Vince's to the moment the young policeman arrested me. I didn't lie or leave anything out, why would I? They asked for the truth, and in my mind I hadn't done anything wrong, and I told them that. Fair enough, taking the hi-fi, the tin and the beer was a bit out of order – and I was pretty pissed off at Craig for chucking Neville's retirement watch, whether it was valuable or not – but I knew Neville and Jane would understand what had happened and I thought there was no way they'd be pressing charges. Once the interview was over, I had to sign my statement, confirming that everything I had told them was the whole truth, and nothing but.

*

After we'd both given our statements that night, they put Craig and me in the same cell. It was just as blank as the first one I'd gone in, with a bench at one end and nothing else on the cinder block walls.

Craig's mum had been present in his interview and she'd urged him to tell the truth as well. It turns out he did, like me thinking there was no way Neville and Jane would press charges, and our basic stories matched almost word for word, though apparently Craig's rendition was a lot more flamboyant than mine.

We thought we'd be appearing in front of the judge in the courthouse upstairs on the Monday morning, but when Monday morning came they told us he wouldn't have time to see us until the end of the week; we'd be held where we were in the station until then. It was an unusual set of circumstances, but we were full of confidence that we'd be getting out as soon as we saw the judge and so started treating it like a bit of a break off work. Craig's mum even came by on Monday afternoon with a radio for us to listen to.

We danced around our cell to song after song and when Bananarama's 'Love in the First Degree' came on, we jumped up on the bench and, bouncing up and down, belted it out:

And the judge and the jury
They all put the blame on me
They wouldn't go for my story
They wouldn't hear my plea
Only you can set me free,
Cause I'm guilty, guilty as a 'jumping bean'

We only made it to the second verse before the young policeman flung our door open and said: 'Keep it down, lads. Your bloody singing's interrupting the trial going on upstairs.'

Craig's mum came to see us every day. She told us that the reason the police had been out waiting for us that night was because Mark Farina had tipped them off. For some reason, after we'd seen him, invited him to come with us to Caroline's, he'd thought it was a good idea to grass on us. Whether he did it because he was already in trouble with the police and needed a bargaining chip, or he thought what we were doing was actually wrong, I'll never know. The worst part was, they'd interviewed him formally and put so much pressure on him that he'd cracked completely and told them everything he could think of. Not just about that night, but about us nicking from the Spar shop and then busting up the school. They offered him a chance to get off without charge if he gave them more on us, so he even fed them stories about Craig and me individually. He told them about the times I tried to take money from those bank accounts; he told them about all the times Craig had jumped the trains to go see his girlfriend up in Frodsham, and some other nicking he'd been doing. It was a disaster. He'd corroborated our story and gone one further, making things even worse for us.

*

The single most ridiculous thing about this situation is that I still had a key to Neville and Jane's. I just didn't think to use it that night.

*

The second most ridiculous thing stemmed from Jane's visit to the police station later that week.

She and I were taken into one of the interview rooms and were placed across the wooden table from each other. Jane's skin was tanned from her holiday and her hair neat as ever, but her eyes were brimming with tears and dark circles lay under them.

'What a mess this is,' she said.

I stared at the table, running my thumbnail up and down the grain, waiting to hear what she had to say.

'I'm just so worried about you. But there's nothing I can do.' She sniffed, then put a hand on my arm; as ever she was caring for me rather than being bothered about what I'd done. I'd been sure she would get it and I was right. 'I've tried telling them I don't mind you being in the house when we're not there. You used to live with us, for goodness' sake. And I said that there had to be a good reason for you going in through the kitchen window, else you wouldn't have done it.'

I raised my head and saw her dabbing the corner of a handkerchief at her eye.

'There was good reason,' I said. 'I needed my birth certificate for getting into the army. That's the only reason we were there.'

'I know, pet. And the daft thing is, Caroline had it in her bag the whole time, all the way over in Greece. But the police won't have any of it. They say it's because someone else reported the crime, so it's not really got anything to do with Neville and me. They say it's more than just breaking and entering as well, that you're being charged with burglary because you took a few bits, and you've admitted to it all freely, so it's the Crown Prosecution Service that's pressing charges, not us. To make matters even worse, I tried to pay your bail but they said there are some other charges you're up against and so they won't even let me do that. It's all really serious.' She took a deep breath, composing herself a little.

'Caroline's just beside herself. You know how she dotes on you still.'

I tried to smile, guessing that's what she needed. 'It's fine, don't worry. I've spoken to a solicitor and he says that when this gets taken in front of a judge they'll see that it was okay for me to be there and I'll be out in no time.'

*

But the judge didn't want to handle our case there and then, and after a week of being in the cell with Craig, our bail pleas were officially refused and we got shipped up to Risley Remand Centre, the place criminals in Warrington were held before trial. It could be days, weeks or months before the judge would see us again for sentencing.

We had to sit it out.

14

ON REMAND AT H.M.P.

RISLEY

*Dr Greenberg: Would you say privacy is
particularly important to you?*

The holding area was nothing more than a cage.
Fifteen or so of us were packed inside, sitting
on narrow wooden benches, not more than
five feet between our rows.

The guy opposite me, short with dark brown hair
and a tattoo creeping us his neck out of his shirt collar,
pulled a packet of Benson and Hedges from his chest
pocket. He fingered the cigarette he withdrew like it
was his last, though I could see the pack of ten was
nearly full, then he clamped it between his lips and lit
up with a cheap, red corner shop lighter. He stuffed
the pack back into his shirt pocket.

He inhaled deeply, staring at the cigarette the
whole time as he pulled it away from his lips. The

smoke drifted across the air to me, to everyone, and made me think about a smoke of my own, but there was no way I was pulling my backy out in this cage.

'Hey, pal,' the lad sat next to the smoker said. 'You got a spare one of them for me?'

'Yeah, alright, Jimmy, but you owe me one.' The smoker pulled the packet out of his pocket once more and flicked open the cardboard lid, knocking up a single cigarette in a smooth, practised movement.

Jimmy took it and the red lighter and sparked up, inhaling just as deeply as his mate. The smell of smoke thickened in the cage.

A guy two down from me shuffled in his seat. 'Hey, mate,' he said, leaning across the lad next to him to get closer to the smoker. 'You got one for me and all?'

The smoker took his cigarette from between his lips. 'No, lad, I don't.'

'Now, come on, I'm sure I spied me at least another five in that pack. Don't be greedy.'

'They're all I've got.'

'Come on.'

'No.'

In a swift movement, the guy on my side of the cage was up on his feet and over to the smoker. He grabbed his shirt collar, lifted him to standing and punched him straight in the face. The crack echoed around the cage. As the smoker slid back down to his seat, the guy tugged the pack of Bensons from his pocket and went back to his own seat, handing the lad next to him a cigarette and then sitting down himself. He lit up and smoked.

Great, I thought. *Welcome to Risley.*

*

After the holding cage, each of us was filed through the admittance process. One by one, we moved into a clinically white room where three officers stood, intently watching us strip off our civvies, checking every move we made for contraband. Once stark naked, it was hands against the wall, bend over and get your arse cheeks as far apart as possible. They scanned for smuggled drugs then sent us on our way to the hatch, where we were issued a starchy light blue shirt and dark trousers. It seemed pot luck whether they were the right size or not. After we dressed, following a quick, lukewarm shower, we were sent off to our cells.

The first time I went through processing, I felt degraded, scrubbed of all dignity. Showing your arsehole to three other men in order for them to inspect it is one of the worst experiences I've had to endure. And it never got easier. Every two weeks I had to go through this, because every two weeks I left the prison to go back to court and try again to get bail. During my time on remand, I must have been processed at least eleven times, if not more – every time I tried for bail, it was refused. Craig gave up going, after a while, but I kept on trying again, and again. I knew it was pointless, but it got me out of the hell that was Risley Remand Centre.

There was a lot wrong with Risley. Two years after I was there, the riots in that prison – over the squalid conditions – became famous, causing the government great disgrace. The prison was built in 1964 and designed to hold just under seven hundred prisoners, all awaiting trial. When I was there, in 1987, there must have been well over nine hundred of us. The men were split over four landings in one block – lads on the top three floors, proper cons (over twenty-ones) on the ground. The women were in a block just across the way – they'd strip off at their windows at night and jiggle around, getting the male inmates opposite them all hot and sweaty.

Conditions were pretty bad. We were supposed to be on twenty-three-hour bang-up, an hour of exercise to break up the day. But that never materialised. The only time the cell doors ever opened was for slop-out at 7am each morning – the time we had to empty our slop buckets: white plastic bowls (the size Dot used for her baking) with flimsy, loose-fitting lids. This was our only chance to stretch our legs, and our only time to see other inmates out of the cells. We'd wake, pack up our bunks so only the thin, dirty foam mattress was left on the bed, everything else folded square in a pile at the foot like we were in army camp. A couple of lads would go outside, before we were all let out, collecting up any 'shit parcels' that had been chucked out of the windows in the night (if your slop bucket was full there was only one choice: shitting in your shirt and wrapping it up as a parcel, then shoving it out the window for the 'shit patrol' to collect in the morning). After they were done, we'd grab our slop buckets and carefully carry them down to the ground floor landing. Sometimes we'd leave our cells and find a ball of bloodied sheets on the landing, congealed blood sprayed across the walls or ceiling of whichever cell they were outside, the leftovers of another inmate slitting his wrists. In the six months I was there, there were six successful suicides from the youth offenders.

For four landings' worth of inmates, we had just three toilet cubicles – all with doors that just covered your middle section, so your shins and head stuck out at either end while you took a shit. There was a row of sinks to get a quick wash and shave, and beside those was the slop-out: a large butler-style sink that we'd tip the contents of our buckets into. One after another, the shit would get washed down a gaping hole in the oversized sink. The stink from it was unbearable, reeking and choking us as we got washed and shaved in the adjacent sinks. Once you'd finished, the screws would move you back up to your cell, not letting you stand around chatting, probably reducing the risk of violence. And that would be the end of our 'hour of exercise' for the day. We'd be stuck in our cells until the next morning, meals brought to us there, quickly handed through the doors, no further contact with anyone but your pad mate.

We weren't allowed to make our beds again until evening, and so would prop ourselves up on our thin foam mattresses, or sit on the uncomfortable wooden chairs at the little table. We'd use our slop buckets when we had to, turning away and trying to ignore your pad mate when he used his. We'd listen quietly to the radio, if one of us had one (I never did), tuning in to Radio One. The other lads seemed to love the Our Tune segment with its depressing sentimentality, though I could never understand why. I smoked all the time. I wrote letters full of nonsense, about the weather and what time I woke up, written to anyone I could think of – mainly Cath, Neville and Jane, and even Caroline once or twice. Cath and Jane would sometimes write back, Cath telling me what she and Jack had been doing and what the latest news was,

Jane saying how sad she was that I was in there, how she was praying that my hearing would come soon and how she knew God would be good to me. I read all sorts of books, from the Bible to Sven Hassle's WWII novels, to Shōgun, whatever I could get my hands on. At other times I would just lie there, looking at the bunk above me, waiting for time to pass, listening to the constant noise around me. And it was constant. Everyone was in a state of upheaval, waiting for their trial dates to come, uncertain of what the future had in store for them. It made them crazy and the din was relentless. Along with the actual suicides, there were plenty of attempted ones too. People would be screaming at all hours, wailing, telling us all how bad life was. Others would be yelling at them to shut up. Someone would hoot, another would holler back. And then there was the noise and screams of fights breaking out.

The screws moved us from cell to cell a lot in Risley, trying to deal with the disruption the overcrowding was causing – attempting to break up unities, which could turn into gangs at slop-out time. When a move happened, you never knew who you'd be put in with. Every time I came back from a bail plea, I was put in a completely different cell with a completely different pad mate. I'd get a real unease running through me as I went through processing, wondering who I'd be put with and how much of a danger they were going to be. We had cards outside our cells – red for Scousers, white for everyone else, and I'd check them before I went into my newly allocated cell. A red card in with a white card meant trouble: a Scouser in with a Woolyback (a non-Scouse). After one bail hearing, I came back in the middle of slop-out – it had been delayed until the afternoon because of a suicide that morning – and I found six Scousers waiting in my new cell for me. They'd seen my white card before I'd even got in there. Three of them bundled me onto my bunk and started punching me. When they'd got their fill, the other three had a go. They left me bruised and swollen, but the screws didn't care.

If you were in with a Scouser, there'd be threats after lights out as well, usually from other cells, hollered across landings: 'I'm going to get your pad mate to knock you out in a minute, lad'; 'You're dead in the morning, Woolyback, going to get you at slop-out.'

Mostly, it was hot air and your pad mate would shout out: 'He's alright, lads, calm down.' But he might try and keep up the threats, winding you up by saying, 'I won't be able to stop them in the morning. They're going to get you.' Nothing much ever came of these night-time warnings, at least not for me. They were empty threats designed to intimidate, to give the Scousers more power; if they were organising something violent, they wouldn't broadcast it. They'd shout to each other in code during the night. They had their own language that, whilst easy to understand in principle (it was a bit like Pig Latin, or the 'Ob' language kids make up to confuse their parents), was spoken so quick any outsider would never have a clue what they were saying. Not inmate or screw. I once saw a lad have his face slammed into the tap above the slop sink, the sound of bone and flesh compressing echoed round the landing – he never saw it coming.

Unlike the outside world, I didn't find it easy to just fit in with everyone in prison. Usually, I take on other people's attributes, that social chameleon, but inside everyone is cagey; a different kind of person from how they are on the outside and, for me, imitating their behaviour was instantly too difficult. Instead, I tried to stay invisible. I was agreeable, but I kept my head down and tried to blend into the white-washed bricks.

Sometimes it wasn't always so easy to blend into the background and lie low; sometimes I had to join in for self-preservation. There was a time when Craig and I came back from a bail plea when twelve of us were shut in the holding cage for hours.

None of us had been allowed washes that day and they hadn't let us use the toilets the whole time we'd been out, so the stink between us was unbearable. Talk started that we needed to do something to get the screws' attention, something they couldn't ignore. There was a space between the cage and the wall of the room and, for some reason, a small gap at the bottom of the cage where the heavy, metal door was. Just enough room to get your feet through. The plan was formulated: in pairs we'd lie on the ground and kick the door as hard as we could. Everyone in there – all twelve of us – would do it, so that no one could grass on anyone else, and if there was any bother after, the screws wouldn't take it out on all of us. The noise was sure to stir the screws up enough to come let us out. The first pair of lads lay down and kicked. The metal door thundered against their boots, but the screws didn't come. After a few minutes, exhausted from the effort, the lads shuffled out of the gap and the next pair went in.

And so on. After a couple more, it got to mine and Craig's turn. We lay down on the cool concrete floor and wedged our feet between the cage and the door.

Craig nudged me and winked. 'Let's give 'em shit!'

And so we did. Our boots thundered against the metal, reverberations shooting up our legs for a few seconds before an almighty crash echoed ahead of us, followed by the prison siren blaring at its loudest.

We raised our heads and automatically got our feet out of the gap as quick as we could, shuffling back across the floor to the other lads on the benches. The door had come clean off its hinges and was lying in the centre of the corridor. Heavy footsteps came running, our usual screws followed by the SOs – senior officers – all in full riot gear, batons raised ready to beat down any of us who were trying to escape. And all that faced them was a group of twelve young offenders and cons, all gathered quietly on the benches, the perfect picture of innocence.

The next court appearance Craig and I went to, the judge dismissed our bail plea, but then went on to surprise us with a sentence of two hundred and forty community service hours. Our solicitor, John Lore – a man who liked like a cross between Elton John and Christopher Biggins, and a useless idiot by the turn of it – straightened in his seat in front of us. The judge told the court to hold. He collected up some papers and promptly left through a side door.

John turned to us, his round jam-jar glasses twitching up and down his nose as he spoke excitedly: 'Don't you see what this means? You're getting out, lads! You must have served enough on remand. He's given you community hours, you can't serve those in prison, can you? You must be getting out.'

Craig and I immediately decided we'd go straight to McDonald's before heading to the pub. We'd call Nick, look up Andrew, get Kayleigh and Nina down, maybe even Caroline and Lisa. Though we agreed we wouldn't be inviting Mark along. It was going to be great.

The judge came back in, papers in hand. The court officials stood and he sat down.

'I hereby revoke the community hours,' he said.

Our solicitor visibly slumped in his chair in front of us. We found out later that the community hours were for criminal damage and were given to each and every one of the twelve of us in that holding cage. We all had them revoked, our sentences still to be served.

'Let the record show,' the judge continued, 'that these hours have been quashed and that the defendants will not be required to serve them upon their release. Return them to Risley Remand Centre.'

15

ALL CHANGE

Dr Greenberg: Do you usually finish your bath or shower as quickly as possible, just to get it over with?

I was at my lowest point in Risley. Never suicidal, that would involve a range of emotion, but filled with how unjust this all was. I hadn't done anything wrong and there was nothing I could do about my current situation. My freedom, which I'd had since I was three years old, was gone. I was trapped in a hellhole. I blamed everyone else in the world for everything I'd gone through in my life, up to and including this undignified, horrendous experience. It all felt so fucking unjust and I couldn't work out why all this bad stuff kept happening to me: Shirley beating me, Adam getting run over in front of me, my old head teacher with his cane, Frank's abuse and mind games, being homeless, Lisa's rejection and Caroline's possessiveness, and now Risley Remand Centre, Mark screwing me over, no chance of bail, and those quashed community hours. Not to mention never feeling a moment of enjoyment. Every day in

Risley was a stress to deal with, unpleasant and difficult. And I felt like I didn't deserve a minute of it. I hadn't done anything *that* bad. Why couldn't I just apologise and try to put it right? I wanted my freedom. I wanted my independence. I was stuck with all these people when I'm a private person, with all this ear-bleeding noise when all I ever wanted was peace and quiet. Being there meant a constant bombardment of stress in different ways, and every second was an internal fight in order to cope.

After around three months, with no view of getting out, my mind started to empty. I adjusted myself by completely switching off from everything around me: the noise, the threats, the violence, the deaths, the constant captivity in one room. I've since read a lot on Buddhism and in reading I have discovered a teaching about meditation: given enough time in confinement, without distraction, your mind has chance to settle, opening itself up to realisation.

It was in this almost-meditative state, lying on my mattress completely zoned out, that my realisation hit me: I was the arsehole. I'd been going through my life wondering why so much bad luck came my way, thinking 'why me?' But suddenly it became clear that I'd deserved all I'd got. Shirley beat me because I was a difficult child who stole money from her. Adam was run over in front of me because we weren't looking properly when we crossed the street. My old headmaster used the cane on me because I disrupted classes and skipped school. Frank came after me because he suspected me of stealing because I had stolen plenty previously. I was homeless because I was belligerent and uncaring towards my mother. Lisa rejected me because I wasn't her type, and Caroline was possessive because I'd said I'd be her boyfriend. I was in Risley Remand Centre because I'd fucked up, broken into the Spar shop, into the school and into Neville and Jane's. Mike had shopped me for some good reason, and I *had* committed every crime he listed to the police. I got the community hours because I'd caused criminal damage, and I had them revoked because I still had a sentence to serve for burglary and everything else. I was the one taking everything for granted and doing what I liked. I was the arsehole not caring about anyone else, hating the world and everyone in it, so of course I was going to get bad luck coming my way.

Lying there on my bed, my pad mate reading silently in the bunk above me, I finally understood that my life didn't have to continue forever in the way it had started; I wouldn't have to suffer every day for the rest of my life. I was going to view things in a different way, keep myself out of trouble and accept responsibility for my behaviour.

In an effort to see things differently, the next time the lad with the book trolley came round our cell I picked up something I'd never usually read, a book about King Arthur. I read all about young Arthur, who had no prospects until the day he wrenched Excalibur from the stone. I read about how he ruled his land with honour, respected by the knights of his round table. It might all be legend and myth, but here were men with principles and motivation, and I considered the life that was being portrayed through these stories. These ideas of chivalrous conduct were centuries old and the men were so very different from who I was. King Arthur was noble and gracious. He was kind, thinking of others and protecting them. He fought for truth and justice; the things I always felt were missing from my life. Here was a male role model that I could emulate, if I chose. And what a coincidence that I should find this book so close to the epiphany I'd experienced. Karma. I was the idiot, but now I could change.

*

A full four months after we'd first entered Risley, I got a white slip of paper under my door in the morning. I was being moved.

The overcrowding in the prison had got so bad they were taking us one by one to a new residential unit in H.M.P. Hindley, near Wigan. I was the first in the block and got allocated cell A1.

Hindley was like heaven. Everyone got their own cell, it was clean and brand new, smelling of paint, instead of shit. There was a recreation area with a pool table, and even a gym, and we were all allocated jobs. If this wasn't a bit of good karma, I don't know what was.

My job was on the loom, making blankets on this massive machine, sending the shuttle across and back again, one of the cushiest jobs there was – though not as cushy as the guy feeding the yarn. It was fascinating, at least for a few days, to see something working like this, something I'd never seen before in my life. And it was so good to be out of the cell for more than slop-out.

Craig turned up shortly after me. His job was serving the tea and cocoa at the end of the day, taking it round on a little trolley like some old maid. He had a great trick though.

'Here's your tea, mate,' he'd say, passing me a mug with one hand, his arm covered with a towel.

Underneath the towel would be a small bundle of food he'd got for me out of the kitchen, bread rolls and bits of meat. He'd pass it to me discreetly, loudly asking if I wanted sugar to cover up any rustling, and I'd stash the bundle away, saving the food for after lock-up, when the screws weren't around.

Christmas came and went in Hindley. I saved up the pennies I earned from the loom and bought myself a pack of small cigars from the tuck shop to celebrate.

Craig's mum came to see him and brought him a radio. It was pretty easy there and I didn't mind it at all. Then, after a month, the white slip came through my door again.

We were due in court the next day for sentencing.

*

Five months after the night of the burglary and Craig and I were back in the cells under Warrington Magistrates Court. Only this time, instead of interrupting a trial with our rendition of Bananarama's hit single, we were awaiting our fate.

We sat on the bench beside each other saying nothing, for a change. Neither of us knew if we'd served enough already, or if we'd be going down for longer, and we sat there drumming our fingers, wishing the time would pass.

About an hour after we arrived, the cell door

opened and I tensed, preparing to head upstairs for our fate. Instead, a screw pushed a young lad into the cell with us and shut the door behind him. Here stood Mark Farina, unable to believe his eyes, not having seen us since he'd grassed us up to the police. The colour visibly drained from his face. I watched Craig grin, like a fox coming across a wounded rabbit.

Here we go, I thought. *If Craig's going to start on him, I'm going to have to join in, aren't I?*

Mark stuttered a few words, trying to apologise, to reason with us, then he stepped backwards, pressing up against the door, not daring to turn his back on us, yet fruitlessly trying to push his way out. As he did, the door was flung open and Mark stumbled back into the arms of a flustered screw whose cheeks were bright red and whose eyes were wide with panic.

'His face!' Craig laughed out, as the door closed again, Mark being taken to his own cell, far away from us. 'Who shuts a grass in with the defendants?'

We burst out laughing and started mimicking Mark's panic-stricken face, the mood of our sentencing nicely broken.

After another hour of waiting, we were summoned up to court. Dressed in my blue denim shirt and jeans I stood before the judge as I had ten or fifteen times before. Our solicitor made the case, put forward all the arguments about age and Neville and Jane and the like, but the judge sentenced Craig and I to fifteen months each, to serve two thirds. Mark got off with nothing.

It was crushing.

A harsh sentence that made an example of us and all that we had done.

We had another five months to serve each. Ten if we got into any trouble.

It was unheard of, our snivelling solicitor said.

We were taken straight out to the waiting coach and driven to H.M.P Walton, in the heart of Liverpool. This was the allocation prison, full of young offenders and cons all waiting to be shipped on to the prisons where they'd serve out their sentences. Usually you'd only be there a few days, and no sooner had Craig and I arrived than Craig was off to Thorn Cross, on the other side of Warrington.

I wasn't so lucky.

Walton was a Liverpudlian prison run by the Scousers, with four pad mates to every cell. As soon as the Scousers saw a white card outside their cell, they knew you were going to do anything they said. Early one evening, soon after I got there, a lad came in from his job and squatted in the middle of our cell floor. He strained for a moment, in front of the three of us, all on our bunks, his face contorted with the pressure, then he reached round and pulled a massive chunk of resin out of his arse.

He unwrapped it from its cellophane and chucked the lump straight to me.

'Here y'are, skin up.'

Now, if you were caught with any cannabis on you in prison – let alone a massive chunk like this – you got six months added to your sentence immediately. There was no leniency, no trial or questions about where it had come from. Just six months added straight off. So I was obviously reluctant about rolling out a fat one. But I was even more reluctant to have my head kicked in by the three Scousers I was sharing with.

I got out my tobacco and Rizla, stuck a couple of papers together and built a joint as fast my fingers could roll, then chucked it and the resin back to the lad.

He sparked up and took a few tokes before passing it on to the other three. The joint finally came back to me and I took a quick drag, desperate to get rid of it before someone walked in.

The lad finished off the last of the spliff then chucked his chunk of resin back into my lap.

'Do another,' he said.

The other two were both staring at me, willing me to disobey. So I did as I was told, rolling it out as fast as I could once again.

Just as I passed the newly made spliff back to the lad, our cell door opened. The screw was a young one, lean and goofy, and usually not much bother to anyone, though you could never know for sure how they'd react on any given day.

'Listen lads,' he said. 'We know you're smoking in here – it fuckin' stinks – just have the decency to wait until we've got off for the night, yeah?'

We all nodded, yeah, breathing a sigh of relief that we'd got him and not some bastard who'd have us all sentenced in minutes.

He'd just closed the door when it flew open again. His SO was there, shouting in his ear hole: 'Never mind until you've knocked off. Cell search, now!'

The lanky one and another PO lurched into our

cell. I glanced at the lad on the floor and noticed the chunk of resin was nowhere to be seen. I don't know if he had an extra set of hands, but he'd managed to ram that chunk right back up his arsehole without anyone noticing. God knows whether the spliff had joined it. They got us out on the landing and searched us, then systematically hurled every one of our possessions out of the cell, so they landed in a heap by our feet – four men's dirty blankets, pillows and mattresses all tangled up together. But the screws didn't find a thing.

Though Walton was a frightening place to be – far harder to survive than even Risley – we at least had time out of our cells. We had recreational time for the gym or on the table tennis, and we spent most of our days working. I wasn't as fortunate as I'd been in Hindley and got one of the most soul-destroying jobs at Walton. Picture the plastic tacks that hold phone cables out the way, the ones with a little nail popping out the back of them. Who do you think puts those nails in place? I got a penny per hundred. At first, I couldn't imagine making enough of them to afford half an ounce of tobacco by the end of the week. But after a day or so I found a rhythm, switched off my brain and let my subconscious take over, and I raced through them.

At the end of each week, we'd get paid and everyone would head straight to the tuck shop to buy their cigarettes or tobacco, their gum and magazines. We'd be let out a few cells at a time and had to wait for everyone to buy their stuff before we could go back to our cells. A couple of weeks into my time at Walton, the screws didn't manage to pay us on time. I'd always been good at rationing my tobacco out across the week, so I had to go a few days without. By the time I got it from the tuck shop, I was gagging for a cigarette and managed to get myself to the front of the lads to buy my half ounce, some Rizla and a pack of safety matches. I sat on the plastic chairs next to the tuck shop, waiting for our screw to round us up, and rolled myself a cigarette. I was about to stick it between my lips to light up when the guy next to me spoke. It was the 'big man' of the block, a huge skinhead who knew how to throw his weight around and who had all the other Scousers eating out of his palm.

'Alright, mate, giusarolly.'

'Sorry, what?' I asked, not understanding his thick Liverpudlian accent.

'Give us a rolly,' he said, pronouncing each syllable like I was dumb.

I held out the one I'd just made, but he didn't take it.

'Nah, I like to make me own,' he said.

Without thinking, I handed Mr Big my tobacco, the Rizla and the matches in one. He rolled himself a fag and pocketed the tobacco in his back pocket, the Rizla and matches tucked neatly inside the pouch too.

'What are you doing?' I said.

'What are you talking about?'

'You've got my pouch of tobacco.'

'No, I haven't.'

A stern look of warning spread across his wide face, but I wasn't taking it. I'd waited days for my backy and

I wasn't going to let anyone just take it off me.

'You have, it's there, I can see it sticking out your pocket.'

'That's not yours, it's mine. Go hassle somebody else.'

Mr Big stood up, and everyone around us turned to face us, watching the scene unfold.

In my usual style, I made a split-second decision: if I let him just take it, I'd never get any peace from anyone, they'd all come after me. I hit him hard, really hard, and caught him right between the eyes.

He didn't blink.

Then he hit me. I fell into the chairs, the back of one winding me right across the stomach. Gasping for air, I wrapped my hands around the chair's legs and swung round, hitting him with it across the head.

Mr Big fell to the floor, knocked out.

Seconds later, I was lying on top of him, the screws pinning me down. I took my chance and delved my hand into his back pocket, retrieving my tobacco pouch. The screws had me, one on each foot, one pushing my thumb backwards, one grabbing my chin, and two on each arm. They hefted me up and carried me away. For the next eight days I was confined to solitary. And I was in my element: I had my tobacco, I had books to read, and I didn't have anyone bothering me. It was great.

When the time came, going back on the block was a bit of a worry. I had no idea what Mr Big would do the next time I saw him, so I kept my head low and was sure not to brag about knocking him out. I never mentioned what happened to anyone. After a couple of days I was still alive, so I guessed he was, very kindly, letting it go.

Then I decided to do some weight training at the gym. I took out all my energy on the weights and, exhausted, shrugged back to the shower room – a communal space where just one or two other guys were getting washed. I quickly showered off the sweat then stepped out of the shower, bending double to shake the excess water from my hair that had grown shaggy in the last few months. Without raising my head, I reached for my towel and started to dry myself off, getting every drop of water, from my head to right in my arse crack.

'Where's me fuckin' towel?' a voice bellowed from behind me. Mr Big.

I looked up and found myself staring at my towel, hanging off the hook where I'd left it, Mr Big's towel quite clearly clutched in my hands, riding between my thighs. I held it out, sheepishly, knowing this was the time of my death.

Mr Big sort of laughed, sort of grunted. 'That's yours now, this is mine,' he said, removing my dry towel from its hook.

I whimpered something like 'thank you' and got out of there as fast as I could. There was no way I wanted to get tangled up in the world that Mr Big ran. There was every possibility that I could if I hung around too long, and, with my disposition for saying 'yes' whenever I was asked to do something, I could have ended up taking a blade to another man's throat. I knew I had to keep myself out of trouble and start turning my life around. Get my karma good. That was the only way I'd be able to stop all the shit from happening to me. And I had a lot of bad karma to make up for first.

Every morning in Walton I waited for that white slip of paper to appear under the door with my name on it. If it wasn't there by 10am, I knew I had to wait at least another day. Craig had got his so quick and I couldn't understand why we – the co-accused – hadn't been sent off together to serve out our sentences. But I looked forward to the day my time would come. Craig had written to me once or twice telling me about Thorn Cross and all I had in store. It sounded like the perfect doss: an open, Category D prison. They were all in single cells, with an actual toilet – not a slop bucket – each. They were allowed to leave the prison for a few hours to do community work, providing they were back by a certain time; Craig's mum was visiting regularly and soon he'd be allowed home on a kind of day-release. They played rugby at the weekends, at the club across the road from the prison. And after, they enjoyed a pint – an actual pint of lager – in the club house. He was enjoying all of this while I was living amongst gangs of Scousers in a prison in the centre of Liverpool. I might not get excited about things, but I couldn't wait to get there.

A little over a month after arriving, I got my slip through the door.

Finally, I'm out of here, I thought as I read, knowing I'd be on the coach by this time tomorrow.

It said I was being transferred to H.M.P. Everthorpe.

Not Thorn Cross. Everthorpe.

I had no idea where in the world this prison was, but anywhere was better than Walton where every moment promised a death threat. The next morning I gathered my stuff up. I folded my blankets into their squares and placed my pillow on top. I left the few letters I'd been sent to rot under the mattress. And then I waited for the door to open.

A scrawny screw came to get me at nine o'clock. He marched down the landing and through to the holding area. I swapped my parcel of blankets for a cardboard box containing my clothes and I dressed in my old double denim.

The screw cuffed himself to me and we marched out to the waiting coach. A handful of lads were already on, none of whom I recognised. My screw and I sat down and soon the coach rattled into motion. Every couple of minutes, the screw raised his hand to scratch the side of his nose. I don't know if he had eczema or herpes, but he was oblivious to the fact that he was yanking my arm up and down with him every single time.

We travelled out of Liverpool, skirted around the Warrington bypass, and up past the north of Manchester. The coach rolled up to Strangeways and we all piled off, into a holding area, where another ten or so prisoners joined us. Then we piled back on to the coach and set off again, joining the motorway and heading north.

Eventually, the coach pulled off the motorway and soon came to a stop outside H.M.P. Wakefield. As with Strangeways, we were loaded off with our screws, into a holding cage, another few inmates came out of the prison to stand with us, and we all got back on the coach together. We joined the motorway again, briefly, then it disappeared and we trundled along roads saddled by field after field after field. The coach was hot and sticky – even though it was January and freezing outside – and the smell of the inmates made the air stale. An hour or so later, we pulled up at Everthorpe.

In the holding cage, my screw already off on the coach back to Walton, I started asking around if anyone knew anything about this prison. Like me, most of them hadn't heard of it before, but the Wakefield lot knew: 'It's a Category A north of the Humber,' they said.

'A maximum security borstal.'

'Twenty-three-hour bang-up.'

'Better get used to it, lad, this is home now.'

I couldn't work it out. I'd been shipped right across the country to somewhere in Humberside (close to a place called Beverley according to the last road sign I'd seen), and Craig – who was doing time for the exact same crime as me, and who, just like me, didn't have a criminal record before this – was still in Warrington in a D Cat., playing rugby and drinking lager at the weekends. It didn't make sense. Our only difference was that he had a fixed address, and I was still, technically, homeless.

16

ONE CELL, SIX MONTHS

Dr Greenberg: *Given the choice, would you rather be with other people than on your own?*

O nce I got inside Everthorpe it dawned on me that the cell I was being taken to was where I would be spending the next four months. There was a sense of security in that thought. There would be no more moving around and shifting from bunk to bunk, sharing with Scousers and fearing for who I'd be in with next. I got a single cell and it was mine. It really didn't matter that I was surrounded by lads who were murderers, rapists and drug dealers.

Now, though, simple silly things affected me. I'd wake up at two in the morning with the thought of milkshake in my mind. I'd drive myself mad knowing I had to wait months before I would have the freedom to walk to the garage and get myself one. I didn't even like milkshake that much. It was the certainty of my confinement that was so hard to deal with. And it all felt so unjust.

People didn't really discuss what they were in for. But whenever it came up, I'd always underplay my crimes, saying something like: 'Yeah, fifteen months in maximum security just for shoplifting. Bastards.' I wanted the others to feel my sense of injustice.

Though I still had the idea, from my epiphany in Risley, that I deserved to be punished because I *had* done something wrong by committing burglary, I couldn't get over the harshness of my sentence. I couldn't get my head around it. I'd never done anything that presented me as a danger to the public. Anyone else in Everthorpe for stealing was there for *armed* robbery. We crept into a house I was completely familiar with and peacefully stole a hi-fi and some beer, then were entirely cooperative with the police. It wasn't the same thing as holding a gun to someone's face while robbing the local bookies. Even emotionless me knew that. Yet here I was.

I didn't have the best start to my time at Everthorpe. I'd been there just about a month and a half when my eighteenth birthday came around. Amazingly, that morning I got notice that I'd have a visitor to see me later in the day. I slopped out and got dressed, wondering who was coming to see me, hoping they'd bring me a big wad of tobacco for a birthday present. To my surprise, when I went into the visiting room and sat on the plastic chair, it was Shirley who walked in. I hadn't seen her since that day down the social services. She looked basically the same, the few years we'd been apart hadn't changed her, and her face told me immediately that she was using all her might to show me she was pissed off and angry.

Cath, Nan and Grandad followed Shirley into the room and they all sat down on the hard chairs, facing me but staring at the table.

'We've come here to tell you,' Shirley said, her voice flat and lacking any emotion, 'that now you're eighteen you can expect never to hear from any of us again.'

My nan shifted in her chair a little, but kept her eyes focussed on the table. She and my grandad were well-to-do, they had pride, and it must have been killing them to be sitting in an actual prison with their convicted grandson. God knows what Shirley had told them I'd done.

'You're a let-down and we don't want to see you again. So don't bother coming round when you get out,' Shirley went on. 'And you also need to know that Shep's dead. He was ill and needed an operation I couldn't afford. Seventy quid, that thieving vet wanted. Les next door offered to pay, but I couldn't take money off him. So I had the dog put down instead. He spent all his bloody time staring out the window waiting for you to come home anyway, useless thing.' She fluffed her hair with her fingers before scraping her chair back and pulling on the hem of her skirt. 'Anyway, that's all you need to know.'

Shirley stood up, I saw her scan the faces of the other lads in the visiting room.

Cath made brief eye contact with me, a look that told me this visit wasn't what she'd wanted to do. Nan and Grandad kept their heads down as their chairs scraped across the hard concrete floor and they filed out after my mother and sister.

Shep had been pining for me all this time, I thought, as I sat on my bed in my cell afterwards. The poor thing suffered because Shirley was too tight and proud to get his vets bills paid. I ran my hand over my left elbow. There were three small indentations there where I'd come off my bike, swerving to avoid Shep as he'd jumped out in front of me when I was on my paper round one evening. I'd dug the bits of gravel out myself, but they'd each left a small scar.

A short time after that, I managed to get myself into some trouble. Everthorpe was a calmer prison than the others I'd been in – all the lads were a bit more stable, knowing they'd be there for a certain amount of time, the lack of uncertainty chilled them out. This less hostile environment meant I got to know a few people – like Paul who had the cell next door to mine and who was from Manchester as well.

He was alright. Looked a bit like Burt Reynolds, with that sluggish moustache and thick, dark hair. He was a real happy-go-lucky sort, always chatting away to anyone he met, but without being too annoying, and never with an ulterior motive. He reminded me a lot of my old mates back in Manchester, a kind of leave-everyone-to-themselves attitude – not like the gossipy closeness of the people I knew in Warrington, who always wanted to know each other's business.

A few days before his release, Paul got a bit rowdy one night and set fire to some scraps of material in his cell. I don't know what had been going through his mind, he must have known the extended sentence that would come his way, but he chucked the ball of burning fabric out of his window and it landed on the grass at the bottom of the wing, smouldering brightly in the dark. He whooped and shouted as he threw down more and more strips of the material, adding to the fire, and all the noise attracted a bit of attention from the other inmates. We all got going, shredding pieces of our blankets and chucking books and stuff onto Paul's mini bonfire. It was a laugh: there was no fear of it catching hold of the building – all I could see from my third floor cell was a warm glow on the dark grass below, no climbing flames and no fire engines needed. But the screws didn't see it as funny and they started to go mental. One of them, a short guy with greying hair who always walked like he'd got a poker shoved up his backside, went charging outside and waved a blanket over the fire, stamping it down to put out the glow. Once he'd finished, which didn't take long, he stood at the foot of our wing, addressing all us inmates sticking our heads up to our windows.

'Who started this fire?' he shouted up, his voice like a sergeant major.

Several people whooped and called out obscenities. A couple of smart mouths questioned what fire, as he'd just stomped the thing out.

'Come on, who started this fire?' he demanded, getting all hot and bothered. Although I couldn't see that far in the dark, I could imagine his cheeks puffing up red the way they did whenever he shouted. 'If you don't tell me right now, the whole wing's getting punished!'

I should have guessed it was an empty threat, but I didn't think. My brain kicked into gear with a question that I had to answer: Paul's getting out in a few days, that would be an end to it if he confessed, I had a good few months left, so should I confess to help him out?

There was no consideration for consequences.

I had posed myself a question and I needed an answer.

So I resorted to my go to: the positive decision.

Formed in less than a second: Yes.

'It was me,' I said, loud and clear. Everyone fell silent. The screw shone his torch across our faces. 'It was me,' I said again and the torch light landed on me.

'Hughes!' the screw shouted, then he strode away from the smouldering heap, making a beeline for my cell.

I stood there in the dark on my own wondering what the hell I'd just done.

I heard someone close by shout out: 'Bloody hell, Paul, mate, that was good of him.'

Yeah, I thought, really good of me.

I didn't have time to think on it more: the screw was at the door, unlocking, wrapping a hand around my upper arm, marching, marching, marching to the governor's office. One screw stood in front of me, facing me, blocking my left shoulder. Another screw stood behind, facing me, blocking my right. I couldn't move an inch without them moving with me. The governor was already waiting, sat in his chair at the head of a long table, a screw stood on either side of him.

I hung my head.

His words blurred into one another as he

sentenced me on the spot to an additional two months. I would now serve twelve of my original fifteen, instead of just ten. In one second, I'd managed to double the time I had left to serve, from two months to four.

Back in my cell, I started to feel sorry for myself. How could they sentence me to an extra two months? But, unlike before, the answer came straight to me and I stopped with the pity: of course I was getting extra time, I just admitted to starting a fire in a prison, for God's sake, what did I think was going to happen?

*

It's only now that I know about the anhedonia that I vaguely understand why I did this for Paul. Any normal person would have thought twice and kept their gob shut.

*

For my final four months, I kept my head down and got on with my time. Now and again I applied for work – I really wanted a farm job that took you off site every day – but I never got anything. Craig's mum came to see me once, telling me they'd moved to a bigger house on Poplars Avenue. Craig was out and there was a bed for me at the new place when I'd done my time. I read books, played pool and watched telly. I went to a few woodworking classes, making a pair of wooden scales (perfect for all the drug dealers in there) and a tobacco tin (which was, essentially, a normal tobacco tin with little wooden matchsticks pasted to every side).

My window faced the prison entrance and, every so often, I'd see someone leave. I soon realised there was a cruel trick the prison service played on some of the cons as they got out. The lad would go through the process of leaving, get all the checks and paperwork done, get dressed in his civvies and escorted to the exit. But, no sooner had the gate closed behind him, his two feet on free earth, than a police officer would quickly appear and slap the cuffs on him, turn him straight around and march him through the entrance gate and in for processing. This treatment was reserved for anyone who hadn't come clean about all their crimes before going inside. If, while they were serving their time, the police found out about other stuff they'd done, then this was the welcome they received upon exit. It kept us all on our toes, wondering if there was anything we'd failed to admit. And a few lads would even come clean about stuff, adding months to their sentences, just to avoid the risk of being arrested when they left. Although Mark had told the police pretty much anything Craig and I had ever been involved in, I couldn't be sure that there wasn't something else. I didn't know, even, what I'd done before prison, if there was anything that could demand more sentence time.

But, when the time eventually came for my release, they stuck me on a minibus with a £20 voucher in my pocket – to get me back on my feet for all of two minutes – and sent me off to the train station, no police officers waiting to pick me up outside. I got on the train at Brough station wearing the clothes I'd worn in the burglary, exactly one year before.

I felt a right div as I got off at Birchwood, in my double-denim that was so obviously out of fashion now. There was an offie across the road from the train station and I went in search of their strongest beer, getting myself a whole crate of Skol Gold Label. Outside, I cracked one of the cans open and put it to my lips. The stuff tasted like engine oil; it was vile and I threw the can into the nearest bin.

With nowhere else to go I headed to Craig's mum and dad's new place on Poplars Avenue.

17

OUT

Dr Greenberg: *Does dancing – or even the idea of dancing – seem dull to you?*

'Y ou out then?' Craig was sitting at the kitchen table, picking at his nails, a mug of tea beside him, his heavy boots up on a chair.

I stood in the doorway. 'Looks that way.' He tilted his head at the chair across from him.

'What's happening?' he said.

'Nothing.'

I sat down on the wooden chair – which I'd last sat on a year ago in their old kitchen – and the anti-climax washed over me. I hadn't been expecting a big fanfare, I didn't expect everyone to jump up from behind the table and shout, 'Surprise!' as I walked in, I didn't expect Craig to throw his arms around welcoming me home like a long-lost brother, but I hadn't expected it to feel like I'd only been away one night.

'Brew?'

I nodded.

He made a cup of tea for me in silence. The sound of the spoon stirring in the sugar echoed around the kitchen. I slurped a gulp as soon as he set the mug down in front of me. It wasn't the best cup of tea I'd ever tasted, but at least I was having it out of prison.

'So you've been out a while,' I said, as Craig sat down again, clunked his boots onto the next chair.

'Two month,' he said.

'Been doing much?'

'Not really. I've not got myself a job yet, though I'm thinking of seeing JP Taylor for some work. Know what you're going to do?'

'No.'

Craig drained his cup of tea.

'Right,' he said, slamming his hand on the table and standing up. 'Let's get you to the pub.'

We went down the local and soon enough all Craig's siblings turned up: Nick, Kayleigh and Nina. Nina had the bright idea of getting me some action – it being my first night out of prison – and she used the payphone out back to call her mate Sharon.

Sharon was a curvy, lovely girl, a real nice personality and a jolly face, but I didn't know her, and there was no kind of physical attraction for me. Even if she'd been the prettiest girl in town, I'd have had to know her for more than five minutes to be able to sleep with her. So I tried to let her down gently. When that ended in a lot of tears, Nina started going on about needing to celebrate and so she dragged us off to the Mississippi Showboat, a club on Howley Lane that prided itself on its cabaret.

A few pints in and a comedy drag trio came on stage. The main guy – dressed in sequins and big lipstick, with a pink feather boa wrapped round his neck – wandered into the crowd in search of a volunteer. My mates, all pepped up now and celebrating my release as only they knew how, started jeering and pointing at me and so, inevitably, I was the chosen one. The guy took me up on stage with him and his two cronies and they danced around me and told jokes, put a wig on me, and, at one point, pulled my kecks down for all to see. I stood there, taking it, because that's what was expected of me; I was part of their show. I didn't feel embarrassment or enjoyment or anger. I just got on with what was required.

When I was allowed back to my seat, I went, and the others all cheered my performance. I sat with my pint, supping up as I was supposed to. But after a quick song, the main guy in drag started coming over to me every few minutes, trying to make everyone laugh by rubbing his boa over my chest, stroking my arm, mounting me. He kept on, returning to me every time he wandered down into the audience – which was a lot – and I let him do what he wanted. But then, after rubbing up against my back and calling out, 'Wasn't it like a baby's arm holding two oranges?' to everyone, he bent down to my ear and said: 'Cheer up, mate, it might never happen.' Then he clapped me on the back and flounced off to another audience member.

I looked around Craig, Nick, Nina and Kayleigh,

and at our other friends who'd drifted into the club, and at the rest of the audience. Everyone was shouting and whooping and smiling. The lad who was getting the drag act's attention at that moment was bright red, visibly squirming in his seat. I didn't get it. I didn't feel any of these emotions that everyone else felt. And I never had.

Soon after, Nina suggested we all go dancing in another club. Dancing for someone without emotion is virtually impossible. I've heard of feeling the beat, but it's utterly beyond me. I told Craig I was just nipping to the bogs and as I walked through the crowd I quickly slipped out of the main entrance, before my friends could see me. I went straight back to Poplars Avenue and curled up on the bottom bunk of Nick's bed – my old bed – completely drained from the day and from leaving prison.

*

A week or so after I got out, Craig, Nick and I all got work with JP Taylor, the owner of a big construction company in the area and a good friend of Vince and Sandra. We toiled for him in all weather, on and off, as and when he needed us. It wasn't solid work, but I took what I could get. In between stints with JP, I worked various other jobs – doing deliveries and other menial things. For a time, I made seafood runs, buying in boxes of prawns for 50p an item and selling them on in the local pubs for £1 each. I had the Latchford run – the hardest place in all of Warrington – and had the pleasure of calling in at the Cheshire Cheese pub most days. Everyone in there knew each other, they were like family, so the day I accused one of them of stealing from my stash, I thought I was dead. I punched a guy and virtually the whole pub crowded round me, pool cues in hand, threatening my life. But then, from by the bar, a big bloke with long hair covered with a red bandana, wearing a biker jacket and leathers stood up and shouted for everyone to stop. They did. The bloke told them to leave me alone, that he'd seen it all and I was in the right. They all turned back to their drinks and games of pool. This was my idea of someone standing up for justice – King Arthur and all that – and I thanked karma for putting him on that bar stool.

As interesting as these jobs were, they weren't bringing in enough to make me comfortable. And so, one January morning when it was pissing it down and I was breaking up concrete for JP, surrounded by people who could barely string a sentence together, I decided I'd had enough of menial work and I took myself off to the local college. There and then I signed up for a government funded electrical engineering diploma – a course that seemed ideal for me, full of practical knowledge, something useful that I could apply to the real world and actually earn some money. It was on that course that I met Rhys, a loud Welshman who was ten years older than me. He was a man's man with greying hair and moustache, and he used to teach me how to say all the Welsh words properly, while I took the mick out of his accent: 'Hi Rhys, are you going up a moun------tain? Is it tiiiiidyyyy?' This mick-taking wasn't one sided. In fact, Rhys prided himself on how irritating he could be, and how easily he could annoy people (I'll never know what he got out of that). It wasn't the best quality, but I spent a lot of time with him, killing time, and he was decent enough.

From the beginning, he'd give me a lift to and from class. Soon after the first term started, Rhys's motorbike was nicked from the college car park and so he had to borrow his uncle's moped for the rest of the course. The sight of us two big blokes on the back of a red and white Honda 50 must have been hilarious to passers-by, him shouting out 'Knees!' every time we went between cars and me gripping on for dear life.

In this time after prison, I dated the girl I thought I'd end up with: Jamie. Short and athletic, a little bit curvy and with blonde hair, Jamie was a real looker and we couldn't keep our hands off each other. She was a good friend of Craig's girlfriend of the time, Stacey, and the four of us would go everywhere together, double-dating, if you like. We'd all go to the pictures, or out to eat, or off on a day trip. In the summer, we'd often cycle over to Moore Quarry – a disused quarry that had filled with water – and we'd go swimming. We'd dump our bikes on the banks, swim across the vast expanse of water, climb up the tallest cliff and jump off, then swim back and dry out in the sun for the rest of the afternoon, before cycling home.

On one occasion, we got back to our bikes and Craig, ever the athlete, suggested we do it all over again. He dived in and me and the girls followed.

I was knackered from cycling, swimming and climbing already, but I kept on going anyway, because that's what was expected of me. But by about halfway across, I began to feel more tired than I'd ever felt before, the muscles in my arms were burning and all my energy seemed to have disappeared. It was a useless feeling, I told myself, I was halfway, what else was I going to do but carry on? I kept swimming, slowly making my way through the water.

By two-thirds across, I had to rest. I couldn't keep my arms moving a minute longer and I stopped in the water, softly treading, catching my breath. The horizon blurred in front of my eyes, went all murky and I took another breath in. It was water.

I'd gone under the surface without realising and my lungs were filling. I gasped again and then, with no more air left in me, and no more energy to help myself, I started to sink.

I remember thinking: *Do something, you're drowning!* And then realising that what was happening was the best, most serene, most relaxing moment of my entire life. I let myself go and let it happen.

The next thing I knew, I was on the bank, in the bright sunshine, coughing; Craig, Stacey and Jamie standing over me. Craig had dragged me out and thrown me down on a boulder, the force of the drop making me cough up water.

Jamie's love seemed to intensify after that day. She and I were virtually inseparable anyway, and Craig used to moan that whenever he drove us somewhere all he'd see in his rear-view mirror was me and Jamie with our tongues down each other's throats; he claimed it made him sick. But, despite this soppiness, we waited six months before having sex. I had great respect for her and knew, when we first started going out, that she was a virgin. Even though she was only seventeen, she'd had loads of pressure from lads in the past for sex, and so was completely amazed that, unlike them, I never once pressured her for it. I didn't understand this: it was her body, why would I want her do something she wasn't ready for? Apparently, most blokes weren't that understanding, and she loved me for it. When we did eventually go there, she was entirely in love with me and we were loosely engaged.

But, almost a year later, I discovered she was never really that into me anyway.

Craig's family were having one of their many parties, loads of people milling around the house, and I was sat in the parlour on my own. Craig came strolling in and grabbed a bowl of crisps off the coffee table and turned to leave. Just as he stepped out of the door, he turned back to me and said:

'By the way, Mike, been meaning to tell you for the last couple of weeks: your Jamie's been seeing someone else.'

And he left, closing the door behind him, yelling something to someone in another room.

I sat there on the plush sofa for a minute, alone, the velvety fabric prickling under my nails as I dug my fingers into the arm. I couldn't get my head around it. My Jamie – my fiancée who I was sure about spending the rest of my life with – had been seeing another bloke. And, to make things even worse, my best mate had known about it and only just told me.

I grabbed someone's pushbike from out the front of the house – my car had actually been stolen earlier that day – and I cycled straight round to Jamie's. She was in her bedroom, just lying on her bed, her parents downstairs watching telly. We went for a walk and she admitted to the affair, told me she wanted him to be her boyfriend now.

And that was that.

For once in my life, I felt something like upset. It was the injustice of her rejection.

I thought we were going to be together forever. I hadn't done anything wrong. I hadn't been a bad boyfriend in any way. I had been attentive and as loving as I possibly could be. But she'd still cheated on me and there was nothing practical I could do to sort the situation out. I tried to get her back a couple of times, because I felt I needed to do something. But it didn't work. Being with Jamie taught me that no matter how certain you are about anything in life, there's always a possibility you could be wrong.

*

On Christmas Eve that year, not long after my split with Jamie, Sandra told me I had to leave their house – right in the middle of another party they were throwing. Craig and I had been treating the place like a hotel, she said, and while she had to put up with Craig, she didn't have to put up with me as well.

I packed my clothes and papers into a black bag and went back down to the party, wondering what I was going to do while having a few more beers. I wasn't bothered about leaving – Craig and I were drifting apart since all that stuff with Jamie anyway – I just needed a solution for my problem of looming homelessness.

In walked Joanne.

Joanne was, from that very first moment, a character. She never drank, but she always seemed tipsy. There was something of Cher about her – big hair, tiny waist, curvy arse, wild dress sense – and she certainly had an edge. She was flirtier than any girl I'd ever met, bending down in front of me in her little white dress, as if she'd dropped something on the floor, then backing her arse up into my face, time and time again. She wasn't the normal type I'd go for, but I didn't care. I had a problem that needed solving and she seemed keen enough to solve it. Once she'd got me hooked, I suggested we go back to her flat.

'We can't,' she said. 'My boyfriend's there.'

I couldn't believe she'd been so overly flirty with me when she had a feller at home, but now I was on a mission to find somewhere to stay.

'Don't worry about that, I'll sort it,' I said, full of determination.

I grabbed my black bags and we left.

Joanne lived just ten minutes away in a housing trust house, split into two flats. The whole walk she pawed at me, telling me exactly what she was going to do to me as soon as we got in.

Her living room was covered in clothes and dirty plates and amongst it all sat a small black dog and Merlin, her short, stocky boyfriend who I'd have to deal with.

Full of bravado – and knowing I had no other choice if I wanted somewhere to stay – I marched into the room.

'Off you go,' I said, indicating my head towards the door I'd just walked through. Merlin looked up at me, his eyes wide.

'I'm moving in,' I said. 'Off you go.' I swept my arm out dramatically towards the door.

Merlin glanced from me to Joanne before gingerly standing up from the sofa.

I hadn't mentioned moving in to Joanne and I didn't dare glance in her direction in case she kicked me out. I needn't have worried.

'I'll leave your stuff round Mum's,' Joanne said, in a tone almost as blunt as mine, and I felt the relief come over me.

Merlin shuffled over to the door. He didn't protest, he didn't even flinch; he just left quietly. Like he'd been expecting something like this to happen all along. I felt really sorry for him, and guilty too, but I had no choice: I couldn't go through homelessness again.

18

A NEW LIFE

Dr Greenberg: Do you find a walk more enjoyable if someone is with you?

My electronics course ended and I passed the exams – building a working miniature lift as part of the test, programmed to stop at floors in the most effective order, working like an absolute dream. But, because Joanne was on the dole (she knew every trick for having a cushy life) I didn't bother trying to get work and just signed on like her instead.

The baby came the following January, less than two months before my twenty-first birthday.

When Joanne told me she was pregnant I was stunned. I had known she wanted a baby, but I hadn't realised we'd been so careless to actually create one. And I knew this was no accident on her part.

Joanne came home from shopping with her mum one day in late April and, as she ran up the flat stairs, she shouted out to me, all happy like: 'We're having a baby!'

She set her shopping bags down on the sofa and started rummaging through, as calm as if she'd just told me about her bus ride. Her mum stood in the doorway, not saying a word, yet not leaving us alone to discuss the situation either.

I didn't know what to say and so asked Joanne if she was sure, and she said she was. She'd done two tests and her mum had seen both of them. Then I asked if it was definitely mine, to which she clipped me round the head and told me of course it was, 'Whose else would it be? I'm not the town bike.' That's when the rowing began and her mum backed out of the flat.

There was never any argument over whether we'd keep the child or not. We were both in agreement that we'd definitely have it. But we rowed about the fact she'd got pregnant in the first place. I felt like she'd trapped me. After all I'd been through in prison, the way I'd become determined to own my mistakes, I knew it was my duty to stay around, and I think Joanne knew I'd have that attitude too. And so I stayed, even though Joanne's moods went from slightly crazy to screaming banshee in the space of a month.

At all hours of the morning she'd wake up and start shouting at me. She'd have a row over going out, over money, over washing, over pots and pans, over her appearance, over the weather – anything she could think to row about. I guessed a lot of it was hormones, but the rest could well have been her personality coming out (she didn't change after the baby was born), I simply hadn't known her long enough to tell – we'd been together less than four months when she told me she was pregnant. The fact was, she suddenly couldn't communicate without screaming. The only respite I got was when I went over to visit Rhys. Though she'd usually come and drag me out of there if she thought I'd been gone too long.

One thing Joanne did manage to do, and early on in the pregnancy too, was secure us a house from the council. We moved just across the street to an end of terrace with two bedrooms and a garden. But Joanne still didn't take pride in the place and within days it was strewn with her stuff again, particularly in the bedroom – the floor deep with clothes.

So there I was, living in a large pigsty with a woman I had few feelings for, getting screamed at every day, and with a baby on the way. But, as soon as Debbie was born, what felt like a duty to stick around changed; I wanted to be there, for her.

It may sound strange, but because I had no emotions of my own I started to feel the emotions Debbie felt. She was so little and helpless. So perfectly formed, yet utterly vulnerable. By taking care of her – cuddling, changing and feeding her – I was filled with the warmth that she was safe and secure. If she was crying, I would soothe her and she would look at me with those big, wide eyes, smiling, visibly glowing with happiness, and that warmed me, for the first time in my life.

Looking after a baby is what you are supposed to do, and so I took to it immediately and without hesitation. I was doing something good because she needed me. Unlike a lot of men, I'd be pushing Joanne to the far side of the bed, to make room for my little Debbie. I'd take her out to the park, all over the place, just to make her happy.

Not long after Debbie was born – just seven months – Joanne announced she was pregnant again. Just like before, I was utterly surprised. I always relied on her for contraception – with my lack of enjoyment from sex, the sheer act of putting a condom on gives my mind time to wander onto other tasks that need completing and then the mood is gone. Joanne was well aware of how I was and I thought she was on the pill. She hadn't indicated that she even wanted more children, especially as her interest in Debbie was next to nothing (she'd rather go out than read bedtime stories).

Chloe came in a whirlwind and I made it to the hospital only after she was born. I was still the first to hold her, though, and to change her first nappy – something I'd wanted for all of my kids. Chloe was just as beautiful and amazing as Debbie and I had the exact same feelings of protection towards her. I still do. It was my job to care for the pair of them and to create a safe, happy and loving environment where they could grow up.

When Chloe was around six months old, the four of us made a trip to see Shirley. Joanne had been badgering me for ages to go, to introduce our children to their nan, and even though I really didn't want to, I gave in to her whining eventually, accepting that maybe it could be good for the kids to know their family. Cath set up the meeting with Shirley for us. Since the day Shirley took me to the social services, when I was thirteen, I'd only seen her that one time, in Everthorpe prison, on my eighteenth birthday. More than four years had passed.

We all travelled down to Runcorn on the bus, arriving at Shirley's at the exact time Cath had said. Shirley opened her flat door as soon as we'd rung the bell, as though she'd been watching out the window, waiting for us to arrive, like she did with Nan and Grandad when I was a kid. She gave me a quick nod. Joanne, in her usual outgoing way, tried to say hello and introduce herself, but Shirley was already off down the hallway and into the front room before Joanne got her name out. We followed.

The place felt eerily like the house we'd lived in when we moved to Birchwood. The carpet looked the same, the lampshades were the same, even the wallpaper seemed to be the same – green leaves running between blue lines – and the old green suite was definitely the one that had come with us from Irlam.

We put the kids on the rug in front of her gas fire and Joanne and I sat down on the old sofa. Shirley sat across from us in her armchair. She surveyed the children not as a doting grandma would, but as though she didn't trust them, as though they could be contaminated with something.

We all sat without talking for a minute or two.

'It's a nice place you've got,' Joanne said at one point, evidently feeling awkward in the silence.

Shirley just kept staring at the kids – Debbie fascinated by the tassels on her rug, and Chloe lying on her back simply watching her sister – no sign of happiness or amusement on Shirley's face.

After another couple of minutes she turned to me. 'What you doing here, then?'

I felt Joanne's hand grip my thigh a little tighter, obviously confused by this strange mother of mine and disappointed I'd been right about not coming here.

'We thought you best meet the kids,' I said. She turned her gaze back to them.

'Debbie.' She stared up at me with her wide eyes. 'This is your nan.' I gestured towards Shirley with my hand and her head automatically turned.

I'd known all along this would be a waste of time, I was prepared for this exact situation – how could it ever have been any different? – but I could feel Joanne's tension mounting next to me.

I let another minute or two pass, just long enough to prove I'd given it a go, then I stood up.

'We'll be off then,' I said.

Joanne quickly jumped up from the sofa and gathered the girls, Chloe on her hip, Debbie in her hand.

'Right then,' Shirley said, without getting up. 'See you.'

And out we walked, back into the hallway, back out the door, back to the bus stop, back to our little house in Warrington.

*

Unfortunately, that wasn't the only relationship that had run its course. Although Joanne was generally an attentive mother, she was now unbearable to live with. Not only did she regularly live up to her nickname of the screaming banshee, but she also refused to stay at home to look after the kids in the evening. All she wanted to do was go dancing. When I had all I could take of her going out every hour, I told her I wouldn't look after the kids on my own any more, thinking that would stop her from going.

Instead, she organised to take them to a babysitter, went out dancing, and then collected the kids on her way home – pushing them in their double-buggy down the street at four in the morning. I had to give in, there was no way I could let her do that, so I relented and stayed in with them while she went out and partied.

The atmosphere in the house got worse and worse between us. Every time she saw me, she would scream at me, flying off the handle if I didn't want her to go out, going crazy if I suggested I go out. And the worst part was, she'd do it in front of the kids to the point at which they'd start crying. I resented her so much for this that I had to do something to change things for good.

In my usual style, I left Joanne at the exact moment I decided that was the best solution. We were all on our way to the shops, to get some formula – Joanne pushing the girls in their buggy, me next to her – when I stopped in my tracks and said: 'I'm leaving.'

Without looking at Joanne's reaction, I turned round and walked back home. She didn't run after me, or shout to stop me. I packed a few clothes into a bin bag and took the bus to the council offices in Westbrook, where I signed onto the housing list. Then I went round to Rhys's.

He was well aware of the situation between Joanne and myself, and he agreed it was probably best for Debbie and Chloe that I left. Not that it mattered to me what he thought. Rhys and I got on his motorbike and drove off to Port Talbot in Wales, to stay with his sister for a break.

After several days of getting some fresh air on the back of Rhys's bike, having lock-ins with the policeman down the local pub, and getting off our faces on whizz and alcohol – not that it ever affected me that much – we returned to Warrington. I stayed a few nights on Rhys's couch before the council got in touch to tell me they had a brand new lot of flats that needed filling and my name had been picked.

For around two months, I refused to see the girls. I told myself it was the best thing for them, that I hadn't needed a dad and neither would they. But as every day went by my decision ate at me. I could feel them pining for me, and each day it was getting worse and worse. I went round to Joanne's.

She answered the door with her hair a mess, a tight top on and a short skirt riding up her backside. Her smile widened as she saw it was me.

'Where have you been, stranger?' she said, quickly smoothing her hair then putting a hand on my arm. 'Come in, come in.'

I stepped into the hall and walked through to the living room. A bloke with neat dark hair was sat on the sofa, his arms folded tight across his wide chest, smart shoes on his feet.

Joanne came in behind me.

'Sit down,' she said. 'Do you want a brew?'

It was like we'd just met, she was fawning over me.

'No, I'm alright.' I shifted my gaze from the new boyfriend to Joanne. 'I just want to see the kids.'

'That's great. They'll love to see you. I'll just go get them.'

'Looks like you're busy, why don't I take them for a bit?'

'Okay,' she said, nice as pie, 'no problem.'

I stood in the middle of the room, the boyfriend glaring at me, while she fetched Chloe and Debbie down, both sleepy from their afternoon nap. We strapped them into the buggy and off I went, a weekend dad with his kids. Protecting them from all the dangers of the world. I strolled round the streets for a while, pushing them along, Debbie chattering to herself and her teddy, and Chloe dozing again where she sat. We walked through the park and then back round to my flat. Joanne hadn't given me any formula to feed Chloe, so when she woke up and grizzled I gave her my knuckle to suck on and it seemed to work.

Ten minutes later, an hour and a half after I'd taken the girls, Joanne turned up on my doorstep. She'd changed into the skimpiest hot pants I'd ever seen and plastered her face in make-up.

'So, how have you been?' she said, sitting as close to me as she could on my sofa.

'Fine.'

Debbie was playing with her teddy bear on the rug, singing a little song to herself, and Chloe sat watching her.

Joanne's hand landed on my knee and started to move up my thigh. I stood up.

'Best get them ready, then,' I said.

I picked Chloe up quickly, before Joanne could

wrap her wandering hands around me, and started busying myself with strapping her into the buggy. Joanne perched on the arm of the chair beside me, her shorts showing almost the full length of her leg.

'You manage okay with them?' she asked.

'Yeah, fine.' I picked Debbie up with her teddy.

'You know, you can have them whenever you like. Any day or night.' Her hand reached out to mine and rested on it. 'I could come round the next time, if you like? Give you a hand.'

'You're alright.' Debbie began to grizzle and I moved away quickly to strap her into her seat. 'I can manage fine on my own.'

19

KNOWING NOTHING

Dr Greenberg: *When you are alone, do you resent people knocking on your door, or calling you on the phone?*

And that was how it went on. I would have the kids whenever Joanne was busy. For a long while I had a job order picking for a chipboard company, but just as I thought I was going to get promoted, I got the boot and so went back on the dole. I hung out with Rhys sometimes, and even saw a bit of Nick Sleden again. I'd do my best to avoid my new neighbour, Crazy Dave – the guy who showed me his psych report the day I moved in, proudly labelling himself as a 'violent, paranoid schizophrenic'. I'd hear him some nights, playing house music and every so often shooting at aliens, screaming, 'Boom! Boom!' at the top of his voice – using his arm as a canon, so another neighbour told me. I once found him sat in the brook behind the flats wearing just his white boxers and talking about 'the frogs'. Another time I came across him doing crane kicks from the *Karate Kid* in the middle of the street, again wearing just his whities.

Sometimes, I'd sit on my own in the flat reading books I'd ordered through the Book Club in Warrington – always choosing ones that were full of spirituality and magic, like *Hallowquest: Tarot Magic and the Arthurian Mythologies* by Caitlin and John Matthews, which came with a stack of tarot cards. This reading was an extension of all that I'd read in prison, of my epiphany and my thoughts on the myths of King Arthur. I didn't mind reading, but sometimes I would just sit in the flat and wait the day out.

The thing prison taught me – aside from never, ever wanting to go back there again – was how to spend time on my own doing nothing. I found I could sit for hours, just letting time pass until the next thing I had to do came along. This probably held me back in those days, at least in some ways: I stopped going out with the lads because I was okay just being on my own. Because of the anhedonia, I had no *desire* to go out, or to do anything. Because of prison I had no *need* to fill my time any more. So I was content to just sit.

And that's when it happened, in one of those moments when I was just sitting, quiet and alone, unthinking.

I was almost drifting off in the dull afternoon light, in what some would call a meditative state. Every inch of me was relaxed and calm. Not a single thought was travelling through my mind: no stresses, no strains, no worries, no judgements or grudges or concerns. Just emptiness. In one moment, my living room surrounded me, with my simple chair and my sofa, my woodchip wallpaper and my thin curtains pulled to. In the next moment I felt my aura expand. That sense of personal space we have around us, that boundary that everyone can feel circling their body, it shifted and was bigger than the room itself. It was bigger than the building, than even the sky. I could feel my aura sweeping around the world, bringing with it an uplifting brightness and an intense clarity of vision that made every molecule in front of me stand out. It was more than just the lights being turned on, more than every light in the town being turned on, more than every light in the world, or the universe.

My brain became two halves, one half positive, the other half negative, and it seemed to me like they both met and cancelled each other out. In the hour that followed, my body experienced so many different and unusual physical sensations that I'd never felt before and that I simply can't explain now. Can't even remember now. I just sat and basked in it for what seemed like eternity.

Then it vanished in the same way that it had come, and I was left alone in my flat.

*

In trying to understand what had happened to me, I read a great number of books on spirituality, including Buddhism, and it soon became clear that what I had experienced was akin to enlightenment. It's very rare for Westerners to experience any form of enlightenment because we are surround by too many *kleshas* – mental obstacles that prevent unthinking – to let go. But, down to my anhedonic disposition and the circumstances of my late teens, I'd unwittingly travelled along the path to enlightenment:

letting go of expectation, taking wisdom from books, being conscious and present, noticing the more subtle details of the world around me, meditating, studying spirituality, understanding the Four Noble Truths, and being mindful. The more I read, the more I understood what had happened to me in that hour in my living room. It's incredibly hard to explain how I felt in my brief moment of enlightenment, but *The Tibetan Book of Living and Dying* does it pretty well. I paraphrase:

A frog that lives by the ocean goes to visit an old frog that lives in a well. The ocean frog tries to explain to the old frog in the well what the ocean is like. The frog in the well says: 'Is it as big as my well?' and the ocean frog replies: 'No, no, it's much bigger than your well.'

'So is it twice as big as my well?'

'No, no, you don't understand, it's *much* bigger.'

'So is it ten times bigger than my well?'

Knowing they aren't getting anywhere, the ocean frog says to the old frog in the well: 'Look, come with me and I'll show you.'

And so the ocean frog takes him to the ocean and, as the frog from the well looks at the ocean, his head explodes.

*

A sense of appreciation, of gratefulness stayed with me for many years afterwards; it was proof to me that there is something more than this life that we're given. And that almost gives my emotionless, problem-solving, water-treading life some purpose.

Soon after, I started working with Nick Sleden at a window cleaning firm – I used to drive him mad with my talk of Buddhism and he'd say, 'You know nothing, you.' To which I would always reply: 'Ah, but if I know that I know nothing, then there is something I know: nothing.' Irritating Nick aside, it didn't take long for me to move up in the company to management. I got married, took a psychology course for a while, and eventually started my own business, which has taken me into a secure future. I've had three more children, and have two step-children, and though my first wife and I divorced, I have married again and life is balanced.

When bad stuff happens, I take it as it goes, never assuming it's happening to me because I'm me, but knowing it's because bad things do happen in life. To everyone. What I try to do always is keep my thoughts pure, free from hatred, grudges and loathing, and my actions chivalrous. I'm sure having anhedonia helps me deal with it all the more easily – I don't have the care or interest to hold grudges, or to retain *kleshas* – but my experience of enlightenment has cemented in me the eternal law of cause and effect: you do something bad and something bad will happen to you.

EPILOGUE

Dr Greenberg: Do people often expect you to spend more time talking to them than you would like?

I met David Hughes when I was thirty-six. Cath had been desperately searching for our father for months and asked me to help. Although I had no desire to meet the man – it would have been useful if he'd been there from age zero to teenage years; I didn't have a use for him now – I realised my lack of curiosity towards him was unusual and that it was different for Cath. She was dreaming of a euphoric moment, assuming meeting him would be some kind of catalyst for change in her life, and so I agreed to help her find him. The first thing I did was call the Salvation Army. I paid the £35 admin fee and told them David's name and an old address Cath's investigator had found for him. Within twenty-four hours they called me at home, just after I'd got in from work in the afternoon, telling me my father was on the line. Would I speak to him?

'Yes,' I said, thinking of Cath.

'I'll just transfer you,' the woman said, her voice light and airy. 'Hang on one sec.' There was a click and a pause filled with the sound of breathing.

'Hello?' David's voice rang through the receiver. 'Is that Michael Hughes?'

'Yeah, it is.'

'Oh, crumbs. I don't believe it,' he said, his Brummy accent strong as anything.

For some reason I'd guessed him to be a Yorkshire man like my grandad. 'I'm your dad. God bless you for finding me. You don't know what this means.'

'Actually, it was Cath who wanted to find you.'

'Crumbs, Cath. What a girl. I knew the Lord would bring us together eventually. And the lady tells me you only rang them yesterday. Isn't that amazing they were able to track me down? It's probably the internet they were using.'

'When are you free to see her then?' I interrupted his flow, desperate to get the conversation over.

He made a brief humming noise. 'I hadn't expected we'd be meeting this quick. But, yes, of course I'll meet her, oh crumbs. You'll be coming too, won't you, Michael?'

'Dunno. So, what day shall I tell her?'

'Let's see, let's see. How's Tuesday next for you?'

'I'll check with Cath and let you know. You best give me your number.'

'Yes, of course. Hang on, I've got a new mobile and I'll just have to look it up.' Excruciatingly slowly, I heard him put the phone down and start pressing buttons. He muttered to himself the whole time, then eventually picked the phone back up and read out his number.

'I'll pass it on,' I said.

'Thank you, Michael, thank you. It's such a gift to—'

'Right then, goodbye.'

'Crumbs, you've got to go. I'll see you soon, I hope. God bless you.'

Three days later, I went with Cath to meet him at the Mascrat Manor pub. It was odd seeing an absolute stranger who looked exactly like me. And that's all he was to me, a random off the street that I didn't care about. He had silver hair and was a bit slimmer, but it was like meeting an older clone of myself.

During our awkward meeting, I asked him why he and Shirley split up, and he diplomatically confirmed what Auntie Mags had said: 'She had a lot of gentleman callers and I wasn't happy about that.' When one of us asked if he'd ever wanted to meet us before, he said he'd tried several times when we were kids. Each time he managed to get our address from an old friend, or from Mags, Shirley would move, so people stopped telling him where we were. Apparently, he spent a few years searching for us himself, until he found a friendly woman at the registrar's office who told him she couldn't possibly give out information of that nature, then promptly left her desk, her big file open with Shirley's details at the top. That's when Shirley moved us to Warrington and he gave up trying. We asked what he did for a living and he said for the last twenty years or so he'd been travelling round war-torn countries preaching to the poor. He'd witnessed undeniable miracles in Kosovo, so he said. He was trying to impress us.

What he didn't understand was that nothing impresses me.

Throughout the hour we were together, he was polite and diplomatic, but he barely said anything without us prompting him. I could see Cath looking more and more disappointed and she later told me that, when I went to the toilet, all he did was ask her about me. It was a bizarre experience all round. Unlike Cath, though, I felt immune to the effects of the meeting. Sometimes, anhedonia can be a good thing: there are no feelings there to get crushed.

I met David twice again after that. Both times he came round to see my kids and both times he barely spoke. I expected that a father who'd been missing his child's entire life would want to put in more of an effort now, but three meetings in ten years isn't trying, in my eyes. Maybe he's the one I inherited the anhedonia from. Thankfully, I find him physically draining to be around – I have no energy to play the game of being nice to him, like I do with other people – and so I don't have a problem with his lack of interest. I still have no desire to get to know him. But, then again, I have no desire to get to know anyone.

*

I never saw Shirley again after that day at her flat with Debbie and Chloe.

Around three years ago, Cath rang to tell me Mum was in a hospice, leukaemia slowly killing her.

'I thought you should know, she's not got long left. She needs a bone marrow transplant and they haven't got a match. Dad's been visiting, though.'

'What's your dad doing there?'

'I don't know, praying at her bedside. He's been going a few times a week.'

'If she needs it, I'll give her the bone marrow.'

Yet another split-second decision. I had no interest in saving her life and having a big reunion. It just seemed like something I could offer to do. So I gave myself a choice: yes or no. The coin toss in my head landed on the usual positive response and so I offered.

'Mike, it's a really painful operation. It's not like giving blood, or having a little injection.'

'I don't care. She can have it if she needs it.'

'It's pointless anyway. She's been refusing all treatment. She told the nurses that she doesn't have any kids. And I think she said her friend who was visiting her was her sister. I've no idea why, but it means they won't be asking Auntie Mags.'

That was an end of it. Shirley died a couple of weeks later and Cath rang to tell me when the funeral was. She also said that I should know Mum had rheumatoid arthritis, which can be inherited.

Well, what a surprise, the only thing my mum ever gave me was arthritis.

She asked if I wanted to go to the funeral.

'What good would that do?' I replied. Then, to try and be humorous because I thought that might help my sister in her sombre situation: 'Have you got a record picked out?'

'What for?' Cath asked.

'To dance on her grave.'

*

So this is me. Anhedonia and all.

I have a moral compass firmly in place, attached to a deep understanding that I never want to return to prison. I avoid anyone who may be 'no good', so that I can't make a coin-toss decision and get myself into trouble. If I don't want to do something, I will just say 'no', though that comes across as cold and blasé.

Unlike my mother, I make sure my kids are showered with praise. I go above and beyond to make them think I'm impressed with their achievements. Because that's what a parent is supposed to do. Positive influence is what a child needs to grow into a balanced adult. My wife reminds me of that whenever I tell her parts of my story.

I still have an absolute sense of injustice in my life, led mainly by the daily battle of trying to avoid injustice while being surrounded by people who enjoy things; I doubt I will ever stop wondering how it is that you can get pleasure from a stack of pancakes, or an Adele song, when I get nothing. All that goes through my head is: why are they smiling at a plate of food; why are they cheering for her – it's just a song? Which translates to: *why can't I feel any of this enjoyment that everyone else feels*? It's just unjust. But at least the word 'anhedonia' gives me an answer to that question; a reason for being how I am. It helps me tread water while I wait for that next problem to come along.

King Arthur, Buddhism and karma all help me get through the day too. I try to live my life as what I call a 'selfish Buddhist', helping people in order to bring myself good karma. Since that experience of enlightenment I've practiced this and it usually works. Bad things still happen, but in more manageable doses. Imagine all the good karma I'm due if this book reaches the hands of other anhedonists, those who still don't have a clue why they're different from everyone else.

Helping people also gives me a bit of purpose in my emotionless life – in one way or another, it means I have something to do that's practical and filling the time. When I gave free psychoanalysis sessions down the pub, I really seemed to make a difference to people's lives, on a permanent basis. They'd be more positive and happy, and I'd get better karma. I really did, life became so much easier to handle.

That's when I thought being a psychoanalyst might actually be a good career for me: it was something that I seemed to be naturally good at. I started the four-year course and within that time I had to take on clinical supervision of my own – self-protection for any psychoanalyst, keeping them from going mad with all the distressing stories they hear. It wasn't something I wanted to do – I don't get distressed – but it was something I had to do as part of the course.

During these sessions, my supervisor started telling me that my lack of reaction to people's problems wasn't usual; my responses weren't what you'd expect from anyone, whether a psychoanalyst or otherwise. This stayed with me, not upsetting me, but lingering in my mind, prompting me to find out more.

Whilst researching a paper I had to write, I came across Dr Greenberg online, through one of our psychoanalysis groups, and I noticed how well certified he was, a respected professional located in America. I decided in a second to try and video call him, to see if he was free for a chat. He was and he was immediately interested in me as a case. We talked several times on video calls, him asking me a lot of questions about my way of being and eventually giving me a form to fill out – grading from one to ten my interest in things, my likes and dislikes, my anxiety levels, how I slept, people's perceptions of me, and so on.

After he'd read my responses, he came back with his mind made up. But, before diagnosis, he wanted to run a series of questions past me.

'Please answer yes or no,' he said. 'And be as honest as you can. Do you think that you could be content living alone in a cabin in the woods?'

*

The night Dr Greenberg told me I was suffering from anhedonia nothing changed for me. I didn't have a sudden revelation that made everything okay. I just absorbed the information, understanding that this label would actually help explain my way of being to other people, should I ever need to explain.

At the end of the conversation, Dr Greenberg had major concerns that I may be suicidal. And I understand why: having anhedonia makes life appear pretty pointless. A life without enjoyment is a life of hanging around waiting for problems and then for death. Everything a normal person does, everything that makes you get up in the morning, everything you look forward to, or plan, is all to do with your wants, needs and desires, what you love, what you enjoy. I wouldn't have any of that, I would just wait for time to pass and exist, if I lived alone. I have a wife and children and I want their life to be as normal as possible, so I try to earn as much as I can so they can have independence and the things they want.

That sounds pretty morbid, pretty depressing. But what Dr Greenberg eventually realised is that I've never felt anything suicidal in my life. You have to care to feel like ending it all. You have to experience some kind of emotion to experience that kind of despair.

If I say I'm scared, I would prefer to not experience the outcome if possible.

If I say I'm happy, nothing bad is currently happening.

If I say I'm sad, I've not found a solution to a problem yet.

I don't feel depressed.

I don't feel anything at all.

Having this condition as long as I can remember makes it glaringly obvious to me how hard it must be to raise awareness. I tried to raise awareness of this condition to help fellow sufferers.

I appear normal, I act normal, I sound normal, one publisher saying to me, 'You look like you have emotions to me.' That's like saying to a depressed person, 'You seem happy enough,' and this guy was in the mental health profession. They say anhedonia is a symptom of manic depression; feeling depressed would be a promotion…

CLOSING NOTES

Although 'Dr Greenberg' represents the real doctor who diagnosed my anhedonia, his name has been changed for privacy reasons. The questions posed in this memoir by his character are based on The Revised Physical Anhedonia Scale (1976) of L. J. Chapman, J. P. Chapman, and M. L. Raulin, published in the *Journal of Abnormal Psychology*, 85, 374-382, and The Revised Social Anhedonia Scale of M.L. Eckblad, L. J. Chapman, J. P. Chapman, and M. Mishlove (1982), reported in the *Journal of Abnormal Psychology*, 94, 384-396.

The Jack Reacher quotes are taken from *Make Me* by Lee Child, published by Bantam Press, 2015, p304-376.

The lyrics of Bananarama's 'Love in the First Degree' have been paraphrased. 'Love in the First Degree' was released in 1987 by Bananarama, taken from their *Wow!* album, London Records.

ABOUT THE AUTHOR

MIKE HUGHES was born in a British army camp in Hanover, Germany, and shortly after, abandoned by his father moved to Leeds, with his mother and sister. After several different places, they finally settled in Manchester. Although he sat his O Levels whilst homeless, with nothing but a pencil he found outside the exam room, Mike left school with a collection of seven pass grades and went on to take an HNC in Electrical and Electronic Engineering. After working in various industries, Mike set up a cleaning company and is now Director of the firm. He is also an author and inventor.

Throughout his adult life, Mike has delved into studies of the human mind. He has qualifications in psychology, psychotherapy and hypnotherapy to mention a few. He now lives in Cheshire with his wife and son, his four daughters all nearby.

The memoir is written entirely from real-life experience. Mike has suffered with anhedonia for as long as he can remember, and was diagnosed with the condition in 1995. 'The Revised Physical Anhedonia Scale' (1976) and 'The Revised Social Anhedonia Scale' (1982) support the diagnosis in this book.

Made in the USA
Las Vegas, NV
24 April 2021